In the
of the Volcano

*x ntelligei Oi   ough
Slums,   the Heart
of Latin America*

Maureen Klovers

The Library
of
The North Shore County Day School
310 Green Bay Road
Winnetka, Illinois 60093

Copyright © 2012 Maureen Klovers

All rights reserved.

For Darwin

ACKNOWLEDGMENTS

I would be remiss if I did not recognize the wonderful people who made this possible.

I owe my pesky curiosity, dogged persistence, and love of travel and adventure, without which the research for this book would have been impossible, to my family. I am particularly indebted to my mother, Mary Klovers, who encouraged me to keep the journal which became the basis for this book, and my sister, Christelle Klovers, who put her red pen to good use while editing my manuscript.

My friend Emily Langer, a very talented writer in her own right, provided helpful feedback and editing, while my friend Mari Sutton, the author of *The Night Sky: A Journey from Dachau to Denver and Back* (which I highly recommend!), provided invaluable insight into the intricacies of the book publishing and marketing process. Mary Louise Pool was a wonderful proofreader.

I owe an enormous debt to the brave, long-suffering, and enterprising inhabitants of the slums of Quito and Guayaquil, who shared with me their tribulations, triumphs, hopes, and dreams, and were unfailingly patient and generous when explaining to me their culture, traditions, and belief system. Many thanks also to those who made my volunteer experience rewarding, including the directors, teachers, and volunteers at the school in Quito, and to the Archdiocese of Milwaukee for providing me with a stipend during my volunteer assignment.

Last, but certainly not least, I would like to thank my wonderfully supportive husband, Kevin Gormley, who persuaded me to persevere through the bruising publication process. I'm very blessed to have found a life partner who shares my interest in foreign languages and cultures, and I look forward to taking him on my next adventure!

AUTHOR'S NOTE

The following is a true account of my experiences in and around the slums of Quito, Ecuador, from September 2002 to July 2003. However, to protect the privacy of the individuals described, I have changed names and some identifying characteristics. I have also chosen not to reveal the exact location of my volunteer assignment, preferring to refer to it as "the Center" or "_____ Center." On occasion, I have slightly altered the chronology of events in order to enhance the narrative.

To the extent that this book contains generalizations, these statements are meant to reflect patterns that I observed during hundreds of interactions with individual Ecuadorians. These statements are not meant to offend, but rather to inform readers and to advance the public dialogue about the causes and effects of extreme poverty. That said, it is important to note that these observations are based on my personal experiences in a very specific time and place, and will not necessarily be reflective of any other individual's Latin American experience. Since 2003, many things have changed: the airport terminal described in Chapter One has been replaced with a modern terminal, the bus system has been revamped, and the incidence of crime has declined somewhat. However, Ecuador continues to suffer from high income inequality, extreme poverty, political dysfunction, and a shocking lack of regulation. For these reasons, as well as the fact that the conclusions drawn in this memoir can be applied to many other developing countries struggling with the transition to a modern democracy in an increasingly interconnected global economy, I believe this memoir remains timely and relevant.

CHAPTER ONE

Darwin lives. I know because I met him high up in the Andes, a couple of miles north of the equator in the shadow of Mount Pichincha. I met Edison too, and Wilson, and even Jefferson.

I am not speaking of *Charles* Darwin, mind you, but Darwin Fernández, aged 13 and (according to him, at least) my future husband. This Darwin—*my* Darwin—had no interest in human evolution or sexual selection, unless sexual selection had something to do with a woman paying attention to him, in which case he was, of course, enraptured.

And none of the Edisons that I knew—and there were many—held a patent. Wilson's mother fervently hoped her country would be annexed by a foreign power, and Jefferson didn't even own a decent pair of shoes, much less two hundred slaves.

I was their teacher.

Unfortunately for them, my teaching experience was limited to a year of moonlighting as an English as a Second Language teacher and a childhood of bossing around my poor little sister under the guise of playing "school." I was really a bureaucrat by profession. Day after day, I sat in a beige cubicle advising U.S. policymakers whether the peasants were really, really angry this time, or merely angry. The former meant that the government might be overthrown, and contingency plans would have to be made. The latter meant that they would riot for a few days and then go home—business as usual and no cause for concern.

It was a little hard to tell from three thousand miles away, of course, but I did my best. I read the intelligence reports. I perused Latin American newspapers. I drew on my knowledge of Latin

American politics and history, gleaned mostly from books written by American academics who had also read a lot of books. I drew on my whopping three weeks of travel in the region. And when all else failed, I guessed.

And then one hot, humid August day, I decided to stop guessing. I was sitting on my front stoop with Orlando, one of the students in my ESL class, and he was telling me how he came to America. "I snuck across the Guatemala-Mexico border in the middle of the night," he said. "Just like America tries to keep Mexicans from crossing the border, Mexico tries to keep Central Americans from coming across. They just aren't as good at it."

I laughed. It seemed so strange to think of Mexico as a country with an illegal immigration problem. But Orlando just shrugged, not particularly amused, and took a swig of water. "I took the bus the next day to Mexico City and from there, a bus to Tijuana. In Tijuana I asked around and found a *coyote*."

"A *coyote*?"

"That's what they call the guys who lead immigrants across the border."

"How much do you have to pay him?"

"Two thousand dollars. Cash. All of my savings. All of my mother's, my aunt's, my uncle's, my cousin's." His eyes narrowed into little slits. "We stayed in a garage for a few days. Then one day he came and loaded us into an empty gas tank and put us in the back of a truck. We were all smushed up against each other. Someone's hair was in my mouth; I had an elbow rammed into my ribs. When we got to Phoenix, the truck stopped and they cut us out of the gas tank. It was then that I realized that I had spent most of the journey wrapped around a corpse."

"What?"

He shrugged again, and a wave of nausea came over me. The only thing worse than spending a couple of hours intertwined with rotting flesh in the Arizona desert, it seemed to me, was not caring about the fact that you had spent a couple of hours intertwined with rotting flesh in the Arizona desert. "Not enough air," was all he said. "They suffocated. It happens."

It was then that I knew, absolutely and definitively, that I did not understand the Latin American psyche, and that no amount of newspaper reading, salsa dancing, or snacking on *pupusas* would make me understand. I had to go there. Not go live in a swanky high-rise in Buenos Aires and teach English to the foreign minister's daughter. Not commune with baby sea turtles on a Costa Rican beach. But really, really go there. I would quit my nice, safe, secure government job, give up my lovely rent-controlled apartment, and spend a year volunteering in Latin America. I would do whatever I needed to do, and go wherever I needed to go, to understand Orlando's worldview.

The question was: where? At first, I was intrigued by the idea of going to Bolivia, the poorest country in the Western Hemisphere after Haiti. But the only opportunity I found involved living in the jungle with some German nuns for a minimum of three years, and there were just a few problems with that: I did not speak German; I had no intention of spending three years away from friends and family; and the one and only time I had ventured into the jungle I had contracted a horrific, mysterious, gut-busting illness that was variously diagnosed as cholera, yellow fever, typhoid, or a parasite. The jungle and I were not friends.

I rejected Chile as too cushy, Colombia as too dangerous, and Brazil as too...*Portuguese*. "What about Ecuador?" my mom asked me one day on the phone. Her co-worker had spent a year volunteering at an American Jesuit charity in Ecuador, and the woman's aunt was a nun who served as co-director of the charity.

"Ecuador?" I tried to remember the last time I had seen a news item about the country. All I could picture was some giant Galápagos tortoises and a lumpy triangle on the map, uncomfortably wedged between guerrilla-plagued Colombia and the lawless Amazon region of Peru. "Is it in the jungle?" I asked suspiciously.

"Nope. It's in the mountains," my mother said excitedly. "Quito. Above the mosquito line. No malaria."

Now I understood why my mother was pushing Ecuador. She had a connection there *and* there was no malaria. My mother lived in fear that her children would die of malaria, or salmonella (no cookie batter for us—it contains raw eggs!), or a snakebite, or maybe even Ebola (after all, Africans bleeding from their pores are only a plane ride away!). She was also very crafty. She knew that once I put my mind to something, there was no stopping me, and the best she could do was steer me to the least harmful alternative. I was, after all, the child who spent most of kindergarten insisting I was Oscar the Grouch.

I had to admit that it sounded like an attractive option. There would be other volunteers roughly my age. I would be in a big city, only a bus ride away from exciting weekend destinations. No one would be speaking German.

And so a few months later, I bought a ticket to Ecuador.

I arrived a little before midnight, on a Tuesday in September, and took my place in the *extranjeros* line. A sea of navy blue and maroon passports, it snaked across the nondescript carpeting. We were the foreigners: dread-locked, hemp-clad environmental activists; Europeans in Che Guevara T-shirts; clumps of pasty-faced retirees clutching binoculars and birding guides. "Mae told me she saw *hundreds* of blue-footed boobies on their tour of the Galápagos," the older woman in front of me gushed to her companion. She wore a Panama hat, a Hawaiian shirt, and purple tennis shoes with a big Nike swoosh.

Her companion sighed and adjusted her camera strap. "Of course, Mae was on the fourteen-day tour. Her husband was a doctor."

They discussed some kind of red-throated bird and another with a blue crest. They whipped themselves into a frenzy over the wedge-rumped storm petrel, or possibly the rumpled-wedge storm petrel. To me, it just sounded like a very unfortunate junior high nickname. To them, apparently, it was major bragging rights in their retirement community. "No one at Whispering Springs Manor," Panama hat woman said in a hushed voice, "has seen one." Her companion's eyes narrowed. It was a challenge.

The wait dragged on and on. The tattooed Israeli girl behind me got into a lotus position and began to meditate, and I amused myself by composing a personal ad for her: *International environmental activist/Hebrew goddess, equally at home in a Tel Aviv club and in an old-growth forest. Must love body art, hemp clothing, and yoga. Must be willing to spend three months out of the year chained to a tree eating, nothing but yucca.*

I moved on to hypothesizing about the two red-headed women clutching copies of *The Purpose Driven Life* and a pair of obnoxiously cute Canadian honeymooners. I was trying to decipher a tattoo in Latin when I was startled by a booming voice. "Next!" I looked up to see a stubby index finger crooked in my direction.

4

I approached the official and placed my customs declaration and passport in his outstretched hand. *"Buenas noches."*

He fingered the warped cover. The words "United States of America" were barely visible, and the edges were frayed. Frowning, he flipped through the stiff rippled pages, trying to decipher the ink that had bled all over each page. "What happened to your passport?" His brown eyes were stern and searching.

"It fell in the Mediterranean," I answered truthfully. I thought about telling him how difficult it had been to dry out my travelers' checks, but something about his face told me not to.

"What will you be doing in Ecuador?"

"Teaching."

The hint of a smirk played on his fleshy lips. He cocked his eyebrow and looked at me expectantly, as if waiting for me to retract my absurd statement. He held his stamp a few inches above my visa.

Do not smirk at me, I wanted to say. I know what I am getting into. I spent my weekends teaching English to Latin American immigrants for the past year. I speak fluent Spanish. I lived in Spain, and I spent the past six weeks backpacking through South America. I toughed out the trail to Machu Picchu, spent a day touring a Bolivian prison, and almost drowned in quicksand with only a few forlorn flamingoes as witnesses to my dramatic belly-flopping escape. You think I can't handle this?

But I did not say any of that. I just raised an eyebrow in response and smiled serenely. The smirk widened into a grin. Guffawing loudly, he pounded my visa with his stamp. "Good luck, teacher!" he bellowed, and the other passport officials laughed.

I walked to the tiny baggage claim area—just three carousels—and jostled for a spot amongst my new compatriots, many of whom looked like refugees from a Milan catwalk: slim and aristocratic, polished and fashionable, the women had bottle-blond hair and the men had dark comb-overs and meticulously trimmed mustaches. Others were short and squat, with bristly dark hair and prominent cheekbones. The former retrieved expensive matching luggage sets; the latter heaved overstuffed duffel bags off the belt. I had only a battered black knapsack and a lumpy red suitcase.

Beyond the baggage claim, the semblance of order disintegrated entirely; every inch of space was occupied by an unruly mob trying to squeeze its way through two little automatic doors. When the crowd moved, I moved. When the crowd stood still, I stood still. It was as simple as that.

Bzzzz. The automatic doors buzzed open and we surged forward en masse. A burst of cool mountain air swept inside, and the roar of the crowd outside filled the room. It was deafening, punctuated by shrieks and whistles, shouts of "*Mi hijita!*" and "*Hermano!*" Then the doors buzzed shut once more, and the roar was instantly silenced.

Bzzzz. The doors opened once more, and I was spit out into the parking lot. For a moment I panicked as my eyes struggled to adjust to the darkness. How was I ever going to find her? The parking lot was entirely without lights, and there was only a half moon. Suitcase wheels scraped my leg, and a heavy-set woman yelled at me to move, but I stood there, riveted to the spot. I had no idea *where* to move.

Slowly, dark shapes began to come into focus. Short, stocky men pressed against the railing, their glittery homemade signs glinting in the moonlight. Women clutched babies to their chest. They tensed in anticipation each time the automatic doors buzzed open. The buzz was followed by a crescendo of disappointed sighs and then, from one corner or another of the parking lot, a sudden roar of jubilant shrieks and whistles, and a frenzied waving of homemade glittery signs. An emigrant son or daughter had returned, and all was right with the world.

Just concentrate, I told myself. It can't be that hard to spot a white woman in a largely brown-skinned crowd. Look for the telltale signs of a nun: the no-nonsense hair, the piercing gaze. Seven years of Catholic school must be good for something.

And then I saw her. Frail and petite, she wore a simple cotton shift. Beneath a helmet of silver hair, her ghostly features scanned the crowd, her brow furrowed in deep concentration. She was nearly as pale as an albino, and her mouth was set in the telltale thin, determined line.

Our eyes locked. She gave me the slightest nod of acknowledgement, and I plodded through the multitude until we met on the edge of the crowd. Towering over her, I leaned in closer, unsure if she could see me.

I stretched out my hand. "I'm Maureen."

"I'm Madre Josefina. Welcome to Quito." She had a flat, slightly quavering American accent, and she squeezed my hand in her bird-bone fingers. She motioned to a shadowy silhouette behind her. "This is Zach," she said, and a tall young man in sweat pants and flip-flops stepped forward. "He arrived on this flight as well. There are quite a lot of you this year. Twenty-two volunteers in all."

Zack pushed a thick shock of sandy brown hair out of his eyes and shook my hand firmly, an affable grin spreading over his face. "It's nice to meet you, Maureen."

Zack and I hopped on the bed of her battered pick-up truck. Block after block of ugly, squat cement-block buildings sped by. The moonlight slanted across jagged spikes of rebar rising up from rooftops, flitted across the cinderblock walls that divided the urban landscape into hundreds of tiny fiefdoms, and here and there illuminated a lone figure huddled in a shadow. Tangles of electric lines stretched above the narrow sidewalks that provided a miniscule buffer between each shuttered storefront's metal grate and the cracked asphalt street. There was not a single tree in sight; there was no sign, in fact, of nature or history or any conscious attempt at beauty. All was angular, sharp horizontal and vertical lines, jagged edges. All was utilitarian. The mountain air was cool and damp, and I shivered in my rumpled shorts and T-shirt as we jolted violently up and down along the potholed road. I wondered how I would ever find my way in this urban jungle; everything looked the same to me.

Zack seemed oblivious to all of this. He was stretched out languorously, hands beneath his head, as though he were laying on powder-soft sands in a tropical idyll. Humming an indistinct melody, he swayed ever so slightly to an imaginary beat. "So Mo—I can call you that right?"—he flashed me a cocky, yet somehow charming grin—"how did you end up coming down here from Milwaukee?" He pronounced it "Milwaukay," as if it were a swanky town on the French Riviera.

"Well actually my parents are from Milwaukee. I live in D.C."

He puckered his lips into an "o." "And what is it that you do in D.C.?"

"I work for the government."

"Mysterious," he said. "I like it."

"And what did you do before this?" I asked.

"Oh, I just graduated from college," he said. "I thought 'Hmmm, how could I postpone the real world for a year while traveling and meeting new people?' When a friend told me about this, it sounded perfect."

Zach laughed and went back to grooving to his imaginary beat. We pulled up to a huge white complex surrounded by a fence that was at least twelve feet tall, with iron bars two or three inches thick. The first floor featured a row of businesses: a furniture shop, a restaurant, a bakery, and a beauty salon. The second and third floors were foreboding white concrete facades; the flat roof was stark against the night sky. A tiny man heaved open the gate, and Madre Josefina led us to the back and produced a four-inch-long, old-fashioned cast iron key. She jiggled it expertly in the lock, and two wide oak doors swung open.

It was not what I had expected. The Big House, I immediately dubbed it. An enormous expanse of gleaming white tile spread before us as we crossed the threshold. On either side, wide spiral staircases led to carved wooden doors and, beyond that, to a kitchen as large as my entire apartment in D.C.

Madre Josefina led us past a dining room designed to accommodate at least forty, a gigantic living room with huge picture windows, and a cozy TV room with mismatched old couches. We ascended another flight of stairs and she led me to a wooden door with my name on it. "Your room," she said and padded off down the hall with Zach.

I opened the door slowly and stood there, dumbfounded. As I had expected, it was plain, with a linoleum floor and a single twin bed. But it was the largest bedroom I had ever had and, for the first time in my life, I had my own bathroom.

Maybe I should have rejected Ecuador as too cushy.

The next morning, we stood huddled together on the corner, heeding Madre Josefina's advice as we anxiously awaited the bus marked "La Marín." "Don't take the bus by yourself," she had warned us. "One of our volunteers last year was robbed at knifepoint four times on the bus." And so we watched and waited, and looked over our shoulder anxiously every few moments.

A pink and white bus swung around the corner and slowed but did not stop. Peering through thick plumes of exhaust, a jumble of brown faces dissolved into hysterical peals of laughter as we sprinted alongside the ungainly behemoth, which appeared to have been rescued from an American junkyard circa 1959. "*Más rápido, niña!*" a short, stout man in a yellowed undershirt shouted at me as the rest of the passengers hooted.

The driver's assistant, a sullen teenage boy in rolled-up jeans and a T-shirt, stood in the doorway and coached us in a bored monotone. "*Corre, corre! Salta! Uno, dos, tres, ahora!*" I felt like an unwitting participant in some sort of sadistic boot camp. Timing, apparently, was everything.

I leapt. A split second later, the driver's assistant casually stepped out of my way, and I landed in the driver's lap. Without taking his eyes off the road, he quickly propped me up with one hand, bringing me face to face with what I would soon learn was the trinity of Ecuadorian bus drivers: a portrait of the Virgin Mary, a close-up shot of freakishly large bare breasts, and a plastic rosary dangling demurely in between.

The assistant held out his hand, and we each deposited two dimes into his sweaty palm, then made our way down the aisle to settle into grimy high-backed seats. Through a small rusted-out hole in the floor, I spied the pavement racing beneath us. This bus really is *especial*, I thought, remembering the sign on the side of the bus, just not the way one would think.

Roaring down the narrow lanes of the ugly modern neighborhoods north of the airport, our bus driver played a game of chicken with the other cars and buses as he barreled onto Avenida de las Americas, refusing to yield to oncoming traffic. The sprawling airport sped by, followed by an outdoor cantina featuring spit-roasted guinea pigs, twirling in all of their chargrilled glory. "Bet it tastes like chicken," Zach said.

"It does. Dark meat chicken." I thought of the time I had tried to eat guinea pig in Peru and shuddered. His little paws had been curled up, and his eyes had looked pleadingly at me. His lips were burnt to a crisp, but I could tell that he was smiling. "You know," I said, "in the cathedral in Cuzco, in Peru, there is a painting of the Last Supper showing Christ and the disciples feasting on guinea pig. For the Incas, guinea pig was considered a delicacy."

He raised his eyebrows and looked very impressed. "No shit."

A reedy-voiced indigenous kid, maybe eight or nine years old, stood at the front of the bus and launched into his sales pitch. "I come here today to offer you this special gum for a special price of just five cents. Try it today and you will see that it is the tastiest, richest, most amazing gum you have ever tasted in your whole life, a party of flavor in your mouth; you will feel energetic and youthful all day." He ran the words together in a sing-song pitch, up and down, up and down.

The kid handed us the miracle gum so we could touch and smell it ourselves, presumably to motivate a last-minute impulse purchase. I looked down at the package. "Wrigley-Spearmint," it said.

"Wow, they should hire this kid for their ad campaign."

Zach shrugged. "Maybe. But the Doublemint twins are hotter."

Humble concrete gave way to the luxury high-rises, parks, and theaters of the modern city, narrated this time by a silver-tongued, mustachioed salesman in a polyester suit. "This special price is the lowest you will ever find in Quito," he trilled as he held a package of ordinary markers aloft. "And the highlighters—in not one, not two, but three different colors—are included as a special bonus." His tempo accelerated quickly. "Ladies and gentlemen, you may think that today I am selling markers. That's right, markers. But I assure you that I am not, oh no, I am not. I am selling hope. I am selling opportunity. Education. Upward mobility. Creativity. Genius. These markers will open up a whole new world for your child. They will make him or her the brightest, most successful child in his or her class, the teacher's pet, the envy of the entire neighborhood, the most likely to attend university, to emigrate to Europe..." The salesman chattered on as we sailed past the dilapidated exteriors of the old colonial section, their peeling pastel facades and rusting wrought-iron balconies echoes of faded glory.

An hour later, after inspecting the magic markers, sniffing the alleged "most decadent chocolate ever created" (Snickers), and being serenaded by strolling guitarists and a troupe of Afro-Ecuadorian rappers, we arrived at our stop. Across six lanes of snarling traffic lay the plain white façade of the Center's downtown branch, a boxy building sandwiched between a corner store and a warren of tiny winding alleys. A diminutive olive-skinned man with several missing teeth greeted us at the door. "*Los nuevos gringos!*" he exclaimed, delighted, and clapped his hands.

He led us up a flight of sturdy stone steps. Slightly worn away at the edge and lined with wooden banisters smooth from the oily fingertips of sweaty students, they reminded me of the Catholic elementary school of my youth. Everything about the stairwell, in fact, reminded me of my elementary school, from the mint-green stairs flecked with black to the sandpaper-like treads to the musty smell that permeated the air. I wondered if perhaps the Vatican mandated these things, or if the Pope had a controlling interest in a quarry of mint-green rock.

The man led us to a small open-air concrete patio. Wedged between jagged gray stone walls, it adjoined a covered patio jammed with foosball tables and tangled with jump ropes. Here, we were supposed to meet some of the children.

"Meet" was not really the word for it; "ambushed" was more like it. As soon as the children spotted us—the new gringos—they surged towards us, booger-covered hands outstretched, tangled strands of thick black hair streaming behind them, screaming and giggling. They were, for the most part, small and malnourished, very dirty, and wearing all sorts of odd combinations of clothes: orange "I love Cleveland" shirts with purple cargo pants; pink party-girl dresses streaked with green (was it peas? a laundry accident?) and scuffed-up heels three sizes too big; brand-new jogging pants with dress shoes and glittery tops. *"Amárcame! Amárcame! AMÁRCAME!"* they shouted.

All of the volunteers looked quizzically at me, the volunteer who supposedly spoke the best Spanish. "What does that mean?"

I had no idea. In five years of high school Spanish, the equivalent of a college minor, four months of studying in Spain, a summer of working at the U.S. Embassy in Madrid, and years of having Spanish-speaking friends, I had never heard such a word. It was the first word out of these kids' mouths, and I was dumbfounded. It was embarrassing, and more than a tad alarming. How was I going to teach these kids if I couldn't understand a word they said?

I looked down at a little girl, her hands outstretched, her face twisted in frustration. She stamped her feet impatiently and flung herself at Zach. "I really am not sure, but it looks like she wants you to pick her up."

Zach tentatively bent down and stretched out his arms. The little girl broke into a smile and crashed into this chest. He encircled her in his arms and lifted her up. For a moment, they stood there, eyeball to eyeball, trying to read the other's mind. *"No, en un círculo!"* she insisted, breaking the silence.

He gingerly turned her sideways, planted his feet, and began to twirl in a circle. *"Sí! Eso!"* she giggled in delight. The mystery was solved: *"amárcame"* meant "give me an airplane."

A half an hour and dozens of airplanes later, Madre Josefina herded us all into the "auditorium" for Mass. The auditorium was nothing more than a cavernous open space at the top of the stairs on the second floor, with rows and rows of long painted wooden benches arranged in front of a stage set with an altar. *"Zacarias, siéntate conmigo!"* a wide-eyed girl in a purple sweatshirt cried, tugging at Zach, who apparently had already acquired a Spanish name.

"No, Zacarias, conmigo!" her rival shouted, clutching his thigh.

"Pablo, ven aquí!" another shouted and led Paul to a bright red bench. Paul was a tall, red-bearded volunteer from Iowa who walked like a basketball player and talked like a football coach.

I was alone and childless, simultaneously hoping a child would choose me as a poor second-choice once all of the popular volunteers were taken and yet somewhat repulsed by the saliva and the boogers and the clothes stained with garbanzo bean mash from lunch. You can't expect impoverished six-year-olds in the third world to be clean, I scolded myself, but deep down I knew that somehow I had. I am a snobby schoolmarm and the kids can tell, I thought glumly as I took a seat at the back, feeling utterly unloved and out of place. It was some consolation that kids sat around me, staring at me wide-eyed, but none wiggled onto my lap.

The Mass was a loud, lively affair. In between readings delivered by the Ecuadorian elementary school teachers in surprisingly halting Spanish, the children's choir belted out folksy church songs. Madre Josefina demonstrated the hand motions to accompany the lyrics, while her younger, sturdier counterpart, Madre Kathy, wielded her guitar like María in *The Sound of Music*. "He already came, he already came, the Holy Spirit already came," the kids sang as hundreds of hands jerked downwards to show a lightning bolt hitting the earth.

When the time came to offer petitions, Padre José pulled hand-written petitions out of a shoebox. Tall and gaunt, he had a weather-beaten face and a raspy Brooklyn accent. From what I had heard, he was a man of very few words. "For my little brother, Juanito, who died. For my little sister, Sara, who died. For my mom; I hope she is in heaven. For my dad, who is very sick." The list went on and on.

Padre José read each one solemnly but without the least surprise.

I sat across from Don Rodrigo, the junior high principal. He was a big bear of a man, so unlike the diminutive Ecuadorians I had met thus far, with biceps bulging out of his lab coat—the ubiquitous uniform of Ecuadorian educators—and salt-and-pepper hair crowning his six-foot frame. I had been told he had studied in Germany, and I believed it. He was a great proponent of efficiency, order, and discipline; dealing with his tardiness-prone countrymen seemed to frustrate him to no end.

Shuffling through the pile of papers, he furrowed his brow. His seriousness was almost comic: he reminded me of a general in an old war movie who poured over maps of enemy lines, and then came up with a brilliant plan for some hapless stooge (in this case, me) to execute. Looking up at me sharply, he crossed his massive arms across his chest. "Señorita Maureen Klovers," he read slowly off a sheet, enunciating each syllable with a cultured, almost Castilian, accent. "It says here you have experience teaching English as a Second Language to teenagers and that you studied in Spain."

"That's correct."

"Would you like to teach religion?"

"No."

"No?" He looked at me sharply. "Why not? The volunteers always teach religion."

"I don't think I would be very good at it, and I don't think the Madres would be very happy with me. My interpretation of the Bible may not be consistent with theirs. And I don't like proselytizing. I think religion is a rather personal matter."

He raised his eyebrows but said nothing. "Tell me what you would like to teach."

I told him I wanted to teach math to the *nivelación* boys, the center's term for boys who had missed significant amounts of elementary schooling but were at least as old as the junior high students. These students received a year of intensive instruction in reading and math in order to be able to enter junior high the following year. The junior high was a vocational school—the boys could study to be welders, auto mechanics, or carpenters, and the girls could study to be beauticians, seamstresses, or salesgirls. The women's rights movement had not yet reached the Center.

Don Rodrigo rubbed his hands together and sighed. "I don't think you understand what you would be getting into. These kids are our toughest to control."

"So I've heard."

"They work all day in metal shops and mechanic's garages and attend school for just a few hours in the evening. They aren't use to sitting still and learning. They are used to being on the street, to fighting. You think you can handle that?"

I nodded and tried to look as confident as I could. I didn't come to Latin America to be coddled, and I wasn't about to make finger puppets with the pre-schoolers all day.

"We try only to have male teachers for these students. They don't listen very well to female teachers."

"They will."

I thought he was going to laugh, but instead was surprised to discover that he found not the slightest bit of humor in what he apparently considered my absurd self-confidence. He just looked weary, tired perhaps by the thought of initiating yet another young and overly zealous American, mentally estimating the number of days until I became the latest in a long line to admit defeat and beg for reprieve. His rough, oversized hands massaged his temples slowly, methodically, as his head shook slowly from side to side. "Maureen, Maureen, Maureen," he muttered, as if talking to a small child.

After aimlessly shuffling a few more papers, he stood and turned to look out the window. The sun was setting over the horizon, casting a warm pink glow on the Big House, the playground, and the giant eucalyptus tree. He looked out over the compound, but he didn't seem to actually see it. He didn't seem to notice that the tree had a little bare spot now that the volunteers had learned that the leaves would ward off bedbugs. He didn't seem to notice the shoving match on top of the slide. Instead, his gaze seemed fixed on something beyond the horizon, out of reach. Like a supplicant before the emperor, I watched and waited, wondering whether the prolonged silence meant he was favorably disposed to my request.

Suddenly he cleared his throat and in a nearly inaudible voice uttered a resigned "*está bien.*"

"*Gracias, Don Rodrigo.*" I rose and tiptoed towards the door, eager to leave before he changed his mind.

"Oh, and one more thing, Señorita Klovers." I spun around. "Our Ecuadorian Spanish teacher has decided to become a nun and needs afternoons off to prepare with her order. We don't have any money to hire a replacement. You will be our new ninth grade Spanish teacher."

I froze. Had I heard him correctly? He wanted a *gringa* to teach a bunch of native speakers their own language? "I don't know if I am the best choice," I protested weakly. "I—"

Don Rodrigo raised his hand in a silencing gesture. "You wanted a challenge, and you got one," was all he said. "Now don't disappoint me."

CHAPTER TWO

I disappointed Don Rodrigo on the very first day of school.

It started off well enough. Armed with voluminous lesson plans and diagnostic tests, I strode purposefully down the corridor of the concrete monstrosity that was the junior high, exuding confidence and authority. I successfully dodged several near collisions with the pimply adolescents as they pinched, poked, and pulled each other, swung precariously on the railings, and yelled at the soccer players on the dirt field below. All in all, I considered my first hallway walk a success.

My first Spanish class didn't go too badly, either. The students listened attentively while I barked my myriad list of rules, although it helped, of course, that Susana, the Spanish teacher-turned-nun, sat in on the first class. No one commented on my accent or wondered aloud why Don Rodrigo had made me their Spanish teacher. It was true that their spelling tests were atrocious, replete with misspellings of the words for "go" and "come," and the reading comprehension exercise was even worse, but even so, I managed to look on the bright side: I knew more than enough about Spanish grammar and spelling to be their teacher. Don Rodrigo's trust in me was not misplaced.

Nivelación was a different story.

Just calling roll was a challenge. "Edison Ibarra," I read off a smudged photocopy, looking up just in time to see a tiny indigenous kid in the back of the room kick the chair of an even tinier indigenous kid. "Hey, you! Stop that," I yelled. He looked up, nonplussed. I took a pen away from a boy in a ripped Green Bay Packers jersey who was carving his initials into the desk, and a

16

rubber band away from a scowling teenager with a three-inch long scar on his cheek and deadly accurate aim. He had managed to send most of our chalk—which I had been instructed to guard with my life, as apparently there was a perpetual shortage—sliding along the base of the chalkboard and then ricocheting off the walls. "Edison?" I screeched above the chatter. I hated the way my voice sounded. It was shrill and preachy, desperate. We were five minutes into our first class and already I was losing control. Apparently I was not as good as I thought at exuding confidence and authority. "EDISON?"

Rubber band boy cracked his grease-stained knuckles and raised his eyebrows. His scar jerked upwards as he snapped his middle finger and thumb against his cheek. *Thwap, thwap.*

"*Usted es Edison?*"

He nodded and snapped his fingers again his cheek again, this time even harder. *THWAP.*

"Do you know who you are named after?"

He rolled his eyes. They were brown, flecked with yellow, and they glowered beneath his bristly black eyebrows. "My uncle," he muttered. *Thwap.*

"Yes, but who was *he* named for?" I pressed, anxious not to let this teaching moment pass me by.

Thwap. "*No lo sé.*" *Thwap.* "Probably his uncle."

"That's a stupid question, anyway," Green Bay Packers boy said. His eyes, half hidden behind a thick curtain of shiny black bangs, had a mischievous gleam, and he had a high-pitched, scratchy voice that reminded me of Elmo on *Sesame Street*. "Edison is the most popular name. Everyone is named Edison."

"Really?" I had never met anyone named Edison before, and it seemed like a very strange name for an Ecuadorian.

Green Bay Packers boy nodded solemnly.

"The first Edison was an inventor," I said.

"What did he invent?" Green Bay Packers boy squinted and looked at me intently, as if it were some sort of test.

"Electricity."

His broad features dissolved into a fit of giggles. "Why invent it when you could just steal it?" he asked, and the whole class laughed.

I marked Edison as '*presente*' and asked Green Bay Packers boy what his name was.

"Jefferson," he squeaked, still laughing.

"Jefferson?"

"What? Are you going to try to tell me I'm named after an inventor too?"

"No, you're named after a president."

"A president of what?"

"*Los Estados Unidos.*"

I finished calling roll and put a few problems on the chalkboard: "264+457" in bright pink chalk; "950-458" in lime green, with the "8" wobbling unsteadily into the "5"; and "25 x 3" in an uneven yellow script that looked as if it were going to fly right off the chalkboard. For the first time, I wished I had paid more attention in Sister Dorine's penmanship class. "She doesn't write like a real teacher," Jefferson snickered, and I couldn't disagree.

A quiet boy with glasses squinted at the board. "What is that thing?"

"What thing?"

"That thing. It looks like a cross."

I stared at the wall, thinking that perhaps there was a crucifix lurking somewhere nearby. But there was nothing on the wall except a coat of yellowish paint and a dusty chalkboard. "Do you mean that?" I asked, surprised, pointing at the plus sign.

"*Sí.*"

"That's a plus sign. Haven't you ever seen one before?"

He shrugged and shook his head. "What's it for?"

"*Sumar,*" I explained.

He looked completely confused, so I tried a different approach. "*Dos más dos son...?*"

"*Cuatro!*" he shouted, pleased with himself.

"Exactly," I said. "That's addition." Suddenly feeling flush, I took off my outer sweater and draped it across the chair.

A tiny little kid with two huge front teeth and a squeaky voice whistled softly. "*Mamacita!*"

I stared at him, more than a little discombobulated. I had never been called a "hot little mama" by a thirteen-year-old before, and I didn't know how to react. Flipping off a burly construction crew is always an option, but how do you respond to a prepubescent boy who happens to be your student? Ignoring him, I surreptitiously glanced at my attendance list to identify my little Don Juan. *Darwin Fernández.* I had a feeling I would be calling that name a lot.

As I looked up, a spitball whizzed past my ear and landed with a splat on the blackboard. The culprit sat in the far corner of the room, swirling his tongue around what was to be the second volley. It was my little desk kicker. Rather than acting the slightest bit embarrassed, however, he just stared back into my astonished face, his beady little eyes flashing back a challenge. "What do you think you are doing?" I thundered. He just sat there motionless, as if in a trance. I scanned my class roster impatiently, loath to admit that I didn't remember this particular boy's name. I shook him by the shoulders. "What's your name?" No response was forthcoming. "Come on, what's your name? You—Jefferson—what's this kid's name?"

"Oscar."

"Oscar, move your desk up here to the front of the room where I can keep an eye on you."

Oscar maintained the same steady, steely gaze, not reacting in the slightest. The stalemate continued as I considered my options. Doing nothing wasn't an option; that would embolden all of the slightly lesser troublemakers in our midst. Moving him forcefully was tricky. If I were able to remove him with a minimum of fuss, I would solidify my reputation as a force to be reckoned with; most of the boys were Oscar's size or smaller, so if I could bend him to my will, it would certainly put everyone else on notice. On the other hand, there was always the possibility that I could be bested by a twelve-year-old, and that would not exactly do wonders for my dignity or reputation.

He only weighs sixty pounds, I told myself. How hard can this be?

I lunged at his desk suddenly, pushing it towards the front of the room. The desk moved in the desired direction, but Oscar did not. Instead, he slumped down in his chair and slithered onto the floor in one fluid motion. I let go of the desk and it careened into the blackboard, sending stubby pieces of chalk ricocheting in every direction, which his classmates found vastly amusing. "Don't be so violent, Maureen," Jefferson quipped. "It's not the chalkboard's fault."

Planting my feet firmly on either side of Oscar's little body, I glared down at him. "*Levántate ahora mismo!*"

But Oscar did not react at all. He didn't flinch, and he didn't blink. He didn't shrug like a tough kid, or laugh maliciously like a bad kid, or tremble like a good kid who suddenly realizes that no amount of adulation from his classmates will compensate for the look of disappointment in his mother's eyes when she is hauled into the principal's office. He just stared straight up at the ceiling, his black pupils dilated and glassy, his chest cavity still. I nudged his knee lightly with my foot. "*Levántate, Oscar, levántate!*" My heart began to pound faster as I shook the lifeless body on the floor. Had he had a seizure? Had he hit his head when he fell on the floor? Did he have a concussion?

Reaching down to scoop him up by the armpits, my fingers gently curled around his sweat-stained Cleveland Browns T-shirt. Suddenly I felt a strong grip clawing at my ankles, forcing my feet out from under me. I had been played. It was all an act, a vicious trick.

It was surreal to find myself in what amounted to hand-to-hand combat with a student. There were no protocols for this, no rules. We hadn't covered this is the cursory two-hour training session. It was uncharted territory. All I knew was one thing: I would not let him pull me down, legs splayed out on the floor, surrounded by twenty hormonal teenage boys ready to inform the world what color my underwear was. My credibility would be shot, and Don Rodrigo would be proven right. He would never again let a female volunteer teach *nivelación*.

I swung my hand around and tugged at his fingers. But he just tightened his grip until my ankles felt as though they were locked in a metal vise. I couldn't believe how strong he was.

"That's right, Maureen!" Jefferson shouted. "You can take him!"

"This is not a fight, Jefferson," I said in the calmest, most dignified voice I could manage as I spit a wad of hair out of my mouth. "I am merely"—I grunted—"getting Oscar off the floor"—I tugged a little harder—"and sitting back in his desk, where he belongs."

But Oscar didn't budge. He just stared up at me calmly as he clawed at my ankles. I stared back at him. We were locked in a silent battle of wills. Listen, kid, I said with my eyes, this is your last chance to do the right thing and let me go. Otherwise this is war. Go ahead, his expression seemed to say. See if I care.

I dug my fingernails into his flesh. It seemed so cruel, and yet he had left me with no other choice. "*Suéltame!*" I hissed at him through gritted teeth, but Oscar gave no indication that he had any intention of letting me go. My words did not seem to register at all, in fact. His only reaction was a slight clenching of the teeth, a tightening of the jaw. His strength was beginning to give out.

His hand slipped and I yanked my foot forward, bringing it down on the arm grasping my captive foot, pinning his arm to the floor. I expected him to yelp, but he didn't make a sound. With my free hand I reached around and slowly pried his grease-stained finger from me. He fought me to the end.

I was free at last. It hadn't really been a victory, but it hadn't been an ignominious defeat either. I crawled under the desk and retrieved a half-pulverized lump of fluorescent green chalk. Twenty pairs of eyes watched intently as I leaned my scratched-up body against my desk, pushed my hair out of my face, and straightened my skirt.

Oscar still lay on the floor. "Stay there if you like, Oscar," I said. "I don't care. No one else cares."

Oscar squinted at me for a moment, confused by my apparent indifference. Then he opened his mouth and began emitting endless bloodcurdling shrieks of meaningless syllables. He pounded his fists on the floor, his stocky little legs striking out at the wall, the floor, the desk, and me in grotesque jerky movements. It was as if he had suddenly been possessed by a demon.

Don Rodrigo came running out of his office. Grabbing Oscar by his collar, he yanked him to his feet. "What the hell is going on in here?" he demanded.

"I'm sorry," I mumbled, staring at the floor. I felt as though *I* had been sent to the principal's office for misbehaving. Stand up straight, I berated myself. Look him in the eye. *You* are a teacher. *You* do not want to be demoted to making finger puppets with the pre-schoolers. But it was of no use; I felt myself shrinking beneath his disappointed gaze.

"I warned you this was going to be difficult," he growled. Staring at the floor, I watched as his loafers turned abruptly and marched out of the room. Oscar's black sneakers barely skimmed the linoleum. I held my breath until I heard the door to this office slam shut. *BOOM.* The chalkboard rattled and the floor shook beneath my feet.

My head throbbed. Why hadn't I taken the easy way out? Don Rodrigo had given me the perfect opening. He had practically stated it was official policy to forbid young women from teaching *nivelación* boys. I could have argued half-heartedly with him and then acquiesced, in the interest of respecting cultural norms, even if the norm happened to be *machismo*. For that matter, I could be in Costa Rica right now. On a beach. With baby sea turtles that couldn't talk back, sexually harass me, kick me, or claw at me. Sure, they could snap at me, but I could outrun them.

I looked up to see Paul standing in the doorway, regarding me with a bemused smile. At last, it was time for him to teach religion. "Tough crowd, huh?"

"You have no idea."

The next morning I stood in the courtyard of the downtown center, watching the other volunteers and feeling once again like a snobby schoolmarm, ill at ease and out of place. Why couldn't I be one of the cool volunteers? Zach had three little girls hanging on him as though he were a human jungle gym; they shrieked with delight as they poked his nose, pinched his ears, and climbed on his back. Another volunteer had her own cabal of little girls arrayed about her on the concrete floor, and they were earnestly trying to learn her cool clapping, snapping, chanting games—the very same ones I had tried to learn in elementary school, to no avail.

I stood awkwardly by the jump-ropers, unsure of what else to do. "Do you like to jump rope?" I stupidly asked one of the girls.

"*Sí*," she said in a monotone voice and plucked a booger out of her nose.

"You're very good. You must practice a lot."

She just stared at me, probably thinking I was the most boring adult ever.

The bell rang. Lidia, an attractive Ecuadorian woman in an athletic warm-up suit, strode into the courtyard and nearly instantaneously, the clapping, finger-snapping, shouting, and jump roping came to a halt. Wordlessly, Zach's girls released their grip and slithered to the floor, the clapping and chanting girls abandoned their lesson, and the jump-ropers leapt right out of their Double-Dutch. In silence they formed six perfectly straight lines, arranged from shortest to tallest, and stood at attention, all eyes on the mysterious woman in our midst.

Lidia proceeded to conduct a roll call, military-like in its precision. *"Sánchez, Sandra!"* she called out.

"Here!" A tiny second-grader in a plum-colored sequin top, mustard-yellow jogging pants, and garish red sandals shouted in English and stepped out of line.

"Chilanguilla, Ramona!"

A solemn fifth-grader stepped to the right as the first girl went back in line. "Here!"

When the roll call ended, Lidia motioned for the line of sixth-grade girls to come forward. "This is your class, Maureen."

They marched silently out of the courtyard in single file. Once through the doorway and out of Lidia's sight, however, the line immediately dissolved. The girls rearranged themselves in a horizontal line, clinging to one another like mourners at a funeral, and trudged up the four flights of stairs to our classroom with long faces in apparent dread of actually having to learn something. Only Dolores, a dark girl with thick black bangs and a few nasty bruises on her face, was left out of this special group. She made a half-hearted attempt to link arms with the girl on the end, but was quickly rebuffed with a withering look. I knew that look, having been on the receiving end of it for much of elementary school. Girls can be so cruel.

Resigned, she fell in step with me and linked her arm in mine. She smiled at me and we went skipping up the stairs. If we couldn't be the cool girls, at least we could be happy. No need to look so solemn. "Are we going to play a game?" she asked.

I was tempted to say, yes, you and I will play a game while the mean girls conjugate verbs, but instead I simply said, "We'll see."

We arrived at the top of the landing. The girls broke into a run, practically clawing each other as they entered the classroom in an attempt to secure the desk closest to Cristina, the apparent leader of the melancholy pack.

"Cristina, you promised to sit next to me," a tall girl with big brown eyes wheedled.

"No, she promised me," another pouted.

"Remember, Cristina, I painted your nails yesterday."

"And I braided your hair."

"Siéntense!" I shouted.

They stopped squabbling and sat down, then wordlessly began inching their desks closer to Cristina. The girls next to her put their heads on her shoulders, and the girls behind her stroked her hair. Cristina acknowledged her admirers with a brief shake of the head, then pulled out a nail file and began to give herself a manicure. She arched an eyebrow in my direction as she blew on a fluorescent pink nail. "Maureen, can we play the clothing game?"

"Yes, yes, Maureen, the clothing game!" her admirers shouted like a Greek chorus.

Carmen, a small girl with a raspy voice added, "*Marco* let us play a game where we would race to the front of the room and put on the piece of clothing that he said in English."

"Okay, we can do that when we start the clothing unit."

"No, let's play it now."

"No."

"But Marco let us play it every day last year. Marco was such a good teacher...."

It was all downhill from there. No matter what I did I was compared unflatteringly to their teacher from the previous year, Marco, who had achieved apparent demigod status. Somehow I doubted that would happen to me.

"I miss Marco," Carmen sighed as we lined up to go back down to the patio after class.

"Yeah, well I miss indoor heat and buses that actually come to a stop," I said in English.

"*Qué?*" They looked at me as if I were speaking Martian rather than a language they had supposedly studied for five years.

"You girls should spend less time on your nails and more time on your studies," I said, again in English.

They looked at me in wonderment. "*La profesora está loca,*" Carmen whispered to Cristina. The teacher is crazy.

I sat in the *nivelación* classroom and waited for my boys to arrive. Class didn't officially start until six, but I had asked several of the students—especially those who had never set foot in a classroom—to come early for some extra help.

At this time of day, the classroom was silent and desolate. Twenty worn desks stretched out before me as I sat behind a simple wooden table, grading papers. It was nice to be alone, to be able to hear myself think. I felt competent and organized—something I'd felt far too infrequently lately—as I noted each grade neatly in my little black book. I can handle this, I told myself, and then I corrected myself: I *will* handle this. Last week was an aberration, an unfortunate bump in the road.

Golden beams illuminated the linoleum floor, which had once been smooth, but was now etched with a million angry little lines chronicling endless hours of combat between student and student, teacher and student; each mark represented a desk shoved or kicked or rammed across the room, a burst of defiance or frustration, a momentary realignment of forces until the battle lines could again be drawn. I smiled ruefully as I glanced over at Oscar's desk, and then at the faint green streaks that stretched from the chalkboard to my desk. No amount of scrubbing had been able to remove them; the story of my year would be recorded as well.

Howling down from the mountains, a cold wind swept through the unheated classroom, rattling the windows. I zipped my jacket and rubbed my hands together for warmth. It never failed to amaze me how cold it could be on the equator.

Juan walked in, clutching a tattered, mud-spattered notebook and a stubby pencil. "*Señorita*," he said in his low, surprisingly husky voice, studiously avoiding eye contact.

To me, Juan was mysterious. Stocky, dark, and silent, with pronounced cheekbones and an impenetrable gaze, he had arrived with his family just a few weeks before to settle on the outskirts of the sprawling metropolis of Quito. Taciturn and obedient, he never smiled, and he never spoke directly to the other boys. I couldn't tell if his silence signified shyness or hostility.

I motioned for him to sit in front of me. "Let's try some flashcards," I said gently, holding up, "1+5."

"*Uno, dos, tres, cuatro, cinco.*" I watched as Juan ticked off each grease-strained finger. He worked as a mechanic's apprentice during the day. "*Más uno*," he said, screwing up his face and tapping the pinky finger of his other hand. Holding out these six fingers, he began counting again. "*Uno, dos, tres, cuatro, cinco, seis.*" He looked up at me. "*Seis*," he said solemnly.

A high-pitched giggle filled the room, and I looked up to see Jefferson and Darwin, my little Don Juan, standing in the doorway. "*Idiota*," Jefferson scoffed. "He counts on his hands like a baby."

"And I suppose you don't?"

"Of course not."

"Well prove it, then," I said and wrote "31+8" on the chalkboard.

Jefferson scampered up to the board and grabbed a piece of green chalk. Biting his lip, he turned away from us and began to whisper under his breath. Finally he wrote "39" in shaky script.

"You counted," I said.

"But not on my hands." I smiled, conceding the point, and Jefferson's face lit up. "What are we doing in Pablo's class today?" he asked suddenly, the mischievous gleam back in his eyes. The boys had taken to referring to Paul as "Pablo."

"I don't know."

"Are we going to watch another Moses video, where all the bad guys drown in the ocean? Moses is cool. I want to drown some people," Jefferson said.

"I told you I don't know."

"What? Your boyfriend Paaaaaablo keeps secrets from you?"

"He's not my boyfriend," I said in my most reasonable, I-don't-stoop-to-the-level-of-a-twelve-year-old voice.

Jefferson ignored me. "I think you have a right to be mad, Maureen. And," he added, giggling, "I think you should kick him out of your bed."

"And jump right into mine!" Darwin interjected hopefully.

I felt my face flush. Thirteen-year-old boys around the world may think such things, and they may even say them to each other out of earshot of the teacher. But no one ever *actually* says such a thing to a teacher. At least no one that I had ever known. "That's totally inappropriate," I blurted out. "Darwin, it is very rude to say such things to a woman, especially your teacher."

"Why? We're getting married anyway."

"We are?" I was intrigued in spite of my shock. It wasn't a proposal, and it wasn't exactly a command either. It was delivered more like a weather forecast in southern California: highly reliable and maybe even slightly boring, but pleasant nonetheless. It will be sunny and warm, with a light ocean breeze. Someday we will get married. Just like that. "When?"

"When I grow up."

"How do you know I will say yes?"

"Oh, you will," he said confidently. "You just don't know it yet."

A few minutes after six o'clock, the rest of the class straggled in. Edison slid into an empty seat and greeted me with a grunt, which was more than I had gotten last week. At sixteen, he was one of the oldest boys in the class, and his rock-hard biceps seemed to have earned him a certain amount of respect. Edison seemed to prefer respect to friendship; he paid no attention to his classmates at all. By now, I had learned his routine. He liked to stare at the tiles on the ceiling and carve his initials into the desk with a dirty kitchen knife that he kept in his backpack. If I upbraided him or dared to suggest that he complete the assignment, he looked right through me. His responsiveness was infuriating. One of his favorite activities was slugging one of the few well-behaved kids and then acting as if he were the aggrieved party. He was sort of like Oscar's doppelganger, only larger, quieter, and if possible, even more menacing. Paul claimed he was psychotic. "I think Edison wants to kill me," he said calmly as we discussed our *nivelación* kids over a strange, but tasty, Ecuadorian version of "American" curry chicken one night. He sounded more philosophical and analytical than alarmed but, all the same, he wasn't joking. "I think he might. But if he doesn't kill me, he'll kill someone else. Definitely. I think he could be the next Charles Manson."

But if my four lone studious kids were worried that Edison was the next Charles Manson, they didn't show it. They just sat in the front row, took out their notebooks and pencils, and quietly waited for me to begin.

Oscar walked in, pinched one of Raúl's ears for no apparent reason, and sat down. Raúl was one of my good kids. Tall and slender, with an unruly mop of curly brown hair, he was eager to please and fastidious about his work. "Oscar, that wasn't very nice," I admonished him. "Why did you do that?"

As usual, he didn't even blink, and I decided it was best to ignore him. I would experiment with the silent treatment today. "Okay, today we are going to have a math contest," I announced and then split the kids into teams. "Raúl has six apples. Jefferson gives him five more. Now how many apples does Jefferson have?"

Fifteen heads hunched earnestly over the desks and thirty dirt-streaked hands shot out as the counting began once more.

"Now write your team's answer on a sheet of paper and show it to me, but don't show it to any other teams. Okay?"

"They're cheating!" Darwin pointed an accusatory finger in another team's directions.

"No, you're cheating!" one of the triplets shouted. They were a head taller than most of the other kids in the class and very, very slow. I could never keep their names straight.

The melee began. Edison slugged Raúl, one of the triplets slugged Juan, and Darwin and Jefferson rammed their desks together at full speed. When I interposed myself between Edison and Raúl, they stopped fighting; as aggressive as they were with each other, I had learned that they were reluctant to risk actually harming their teacher. The problem with this technique was that as soon as I ended one fistfight, another erupted in a different corner of the room. It was like trying to dam a river that merely responded by changing course, and today was no exception. I swung around to interpose myself between one of the triplets and Juan, who were now wrestling on the floor, only to have the fistfight between Edison and Raúl begin anew.

The sound of metal scraping against metal intensified over the shouting and the gentle thud of fists on flesh. "*Marido*," I called over my shoulder to Darwin, as I grasped each of Edison and Raúl's wrists and held them apart, "if you don't stop ramming into Jefferson, I'm divorcing you." It was a desperate measure and one that surely would have landed me in the hot seat at a PTA meeting in, say, Iowa. But I had tried everything else and failed. People justified a lot in the name of maintaining order: wiretapping, targeted assassinations, torture. Was it really *that* bad to imply that Darwin and I would enjoy a life of eternal wedded bliss if only he gave up his desk-ramming habit? He would forget about our impending nuptials by the time he was eighteen, right?

To my surprise, the gambit paid off. "Fine," he grunted, and the screeching stopped.

"*Gracias, marido.*" Darwin beamed, and I pulled Edison and Raúl across the room with me. Careful to keep them at arm's length, I arched my back and leaned my lower body between Juan and the triplet. They stopped fighting too. Finally, I thought, we can actually get back to learning.

But it was not to be. A few moments later, Oscar leaned over and bit Raúl on the neck.

"OWWW!" Raúl yelped.

I leaned over and peered at his neck, which was swollen with a ring of crimson blotches. Oscar did not look concerned in the least. I glared at him and pointed at the door. "Go to Madre Kathy's office. Now."

Oscar didn't go anywhere, of course. He stayed, he looked at me calmly, and then he opened his mouth and emitted one of his bloodcurdling screams. I stared into his impenetrable black orbs. Just what exactly was wrong with this kid?

And then there was no time to ponder. The fights erupted once more, the kids began ramming their desks together again, and Oscar, in some sort of bizarre act of spitefulness, even managed to eat our precious chalk. I hope he gets sick, I found myself praying silently. At least it would give me a few days of peace. And maybe he would learn his lesson.

Don Rodrigo appeared in the doorway. His face was flushed, and a thick blue vein throbbed above his left eye. He crossed his thick arms over his chest and shook his head. I had disappointed him yet again. In less than two weeks. *"Mano dura,* Maureen. *Mano dura,"* he admonished me in his stern, gravelly voice. Rule with an iron fist, in essence.

Don Rodrigo hauled three-quarters of my class into his office for a stern lecture and I finished the class with only five boys. When Paul relieved me, I sprinted out of the room, down the corridor and down the stairs, across the pitiful soccer field and past the playground, up the grandiose spiral staircase of the Big House and into the TV room, where I flung myself on the couch. I felt drained of all energy, incapable of uttering a single coherent thought. I grunted at Jeannie, a petite volunteer from Kansas City, as she sat transfixed by "Are You Hot?," a mindless TV show in which the cruel and heartless judges use laser pointers to indicate cellulite deposits on the contestants' thighs. "How was your day?" she mumbled as the smarmy judge circled a tiny area above a hapless brunette's knee.

"Horrible. Yours?"

"Fucking horrible. I think I want to be sterilized."

"Mmm-hmmm."

We sat there in a strange, silent kinship. It was comforting to know that, somewhere in the world, people's greatest concern was an invisible lump of fat.

CHAPTER THREE

"In case we die," Jeannie announced cheerfully as she handed me a clipboard.

"Huh?"

"It's a passenger list in case the bus goes over a cliff. Comforting, isn't it?"

The previous week, the Quito paper had reported that a bus carrying more than forty passengers had driven right off the mountain on the way to Otavalo. Like self-appointed tour guides with a flair for the macabre, Ecuadorian passengers had assiduously pointed out the vehicle's rotting carcass to a few of the volunteers as their bus creaked and wheezed up the same mountain's treacherous sinews a few days later.

Wondering what our chances were, I squinted at the mountains in the distance, scanning the horizon for some sort of sign of just where Jeannie and I stood with Him today. I looked for intense rays of light bursting forth from the heavens like some sort of after-the-flood depiction, or ominous clouds, or vultures circling, but I saw nothing except rows of inscrutable purple mountains silhouetted against yet more distant rows of purple mountains. I consoled myself that God probably wouldn't let us die so close to the beginning of the year with so much work yet undone; He would try to get a return on his investment first. I looked down at the list. María Carmen de las Flores León, Jeannie had written, and beneath that, Ximena Calderón de Burgos.

"I wrote your name down already. Pass it to the people in front of us." A tiny wrinkled hand brushed the top of the seat and I obliged.

"Who am I?"

"María Carmen."

"Oh." I imagined my parents' confusion when they discovered that I had disappeared into thin air on a weekend trip to Riobamba. I pictured a mustachioed, beady-eyed functionary perusing a list of the passengers on the bus that now lay in a smoldering heap at the bottom of a gorge, imperiously informing my mother with a self-satisfied smirk that she was mistaken; only Ecuadorians had perished. If pressed, he might allow that a few could have been foreigners. The aristocratically named María Carmen and Ximena, for instance, seemed more like characters that had escaped off the pages of Don Quixote than Ecuadorian peasants. In any case, though, they were probably Argentines or Spaniards on holiday. Definitely not Americans.

Riobamba. The Spanish word for river and the Quichua word for a plain, fused together, two words that spoke volumes about where the two great clashing cultures of this place had been, where they were going, and what they valued. The Spanish were the people of the river, of that swift-moving conduit to the land and the gold and the Indians just beyond the horizon, and to the rubber and the cacao beyond that, and to the innumerable riches that spread even further beyond, seemingly stretching to eternity. The Quichua were the people of the plain, the heirs of a vast empire laid to waste, a once proud and often restive people now dulled into submission, their daily activities—once vigorous assertions of man's dominion over the earth, expressed in vast irrigation networks and cities—subsumed into the measured rhythms of the earth and the monotony of the agricultural cycle, until they became all but invisible.

The faces of our fellow passengers reflected this fusion—not the sort of fusion that describes a meeting of the minds, or the harmonious blending of cultures, but rather something forced and violent, unnatural even, like atoms ricocheting off each other at warp speed. They were the color of burnt chestnuts, cinnamon, coffee, and every hue in between, the varying proportions of Spanish blood the result of centuries of wars, enslavement, displacements, rapes, and the rare love story. Even so, no one on that bus could have passed for Spanish. Those people did not travel on buses.

31

Jeannie and I were the only gringos on the bus. She had just dyed her blond hair jet black ("I feel safer this way," she confided), so I was the lone light-haired, glaringly white passenger. We were on a last-minute lark to Riobamba, a small colonial city smack in the center of Ecuador, to enjoy our three-day All Saints' Day/Day of the Dead weekend. It was a much-needed break from the noise and dust of the city and the long days of whiny children.

Jeannie skimmed her *Lonely Planet* guide while I rolled the names of the towns we passed off my tongue: Machachi, Cotopaxi, Latacunga. The names conjured up playgrounds for jealous and impetuous gods, ancient rituals stretching back to the dawn of history. The brooding purple mountains fit right in with this vision; the more prosaic concrete block buildings did not.

As we cruised down the Panamericana—the "superhighway of Latin America," paved throughout Ecuador, but only one lane each way, no shoulder—we encountered three military checkpoints. At each checkpoint, the driver's assistant would leap gracefully off the bus as it slowed to five miles an hour, a driver's license and three or four crisp dollar bills in hand, and return with just the license. "That's a pretty good racket," Jeannie observed, and I had to agree.

Riobamba turned out to be just the way *Lonely Planet* described it—a sleepy provincial capital packed with colonial architecture and carefully manicured pocket-sized plazas, all in the shadow of the hulking, normally fog-enshrouded Mount Chimborazo. We spent an hour in the town's supposedly famous religious art museum, where we got our fill of bloody, gem-encrusted statues of Christ, then ambled through the city's parks and squares, peeked in a few churches, and took a few photos of Mount Chimborazo's summit, barely visible through the clouds, just as the sun set.

Later that night, in our hotel room, we lay propped up on our elbows, regaling each other with slightly exaggerated accounts of our college exploits, making bets on which volunteers would end up dating, and sharing our anxieties about the months to come. Our conversation veered from the philosophical to the ridiculous, from God's involvement in everyday affairs, to the reasons our students couldn't or wouldn't learn, to Christina Aguilera's laughable sudden affinity for her Ecuadorian roots. We watched bad Latin music videos and ate junk food.

"I'm glad we're friends," Jeannie yawned as she turned out the light.

"Me too," I mumbled as I turned over. "Goodnight, Ximena."
"Good night, María Carmen."

Sunlight streamed through the windows and danced across my toes. I rose, eked out the best shower I could from the temperamental plumbing, and headed off for my rendezvous with the mountain. Jeannie slept soundly through my morning routine, turning over and grunting a few times, then mumbling a "have a good time" as I strode out the door.

I arrived at the meeting point, a once-grand hotel whose golden years were long past, at seven o'clock, the appointed meeting time. While I waited, I traced my finger over the yellowed map taped to the wall, along a winding road headed out of town, through tiny hamlets, and into rugged terrain, finally arriving at a great bulge in the earth's crust called Chimborazo. And what a bulge it was. By virtue of its location less than one hundred miles south of the equator, where the planet's crust is further from the center of the earth than at any other latitude, Chimborazo's summit is further from the earth's core than any other mountaintop.

My goal was not to reach the summit. Instead, I had joined an Ecuadorian guide and a Dutch couple on a hike to the first refuge. The guide had warned us not to arrive late, as by ten o'clock clouds would descend over the summit, obscuring our view. I stared at the clock on the wall and watched as the hands flew past seven-fifteen, then seven-twenty. There was no guide and no Dutch people. But the sun was still shining brightly; I wasn't worried.

At last our little group assembled. We ambled out of town in the guide's weather-beaten pick-up truck and stopped at the next little town to buy water and snacks. From there, we meandered through ever more desolate mountains. My conviction that the weather would hold began to waver as the first snowflakes fell.

We pulled off the road onto a dirt track and finally onto a stretch of silent undulating whiteness beneath an angry sky. The landscape was a barren wilderness, bereft of trees or shrubs or streams, punctuated only by a few bewildered llamas. No one spoke. When the truck came to a halt, we piled out, shivering, and stole meek glances at the sky. The guide led us blithely onwards into the thin mountain air.

I soon lagged behind. It was difficult to get my footing on the slippery trail, now buried in three or four inches of snow. I'd take a step and slide half a step backward, then repeat, even as my lungs told me that at 16,000 feet I could ill afford the extra exertion.

As I stumbled on into the gray mist, I scanned the horizon for the vaguest outline of a peak. But there was none to be found. Shrouded in mystery, Chimborazo concealed herself beneath a thick velvety fog.

Woman of Ice, Ice Throne of God, Mountain of Ice: these were the commonly accepted translations of the indigenous term Chimborazo; the ancients may have sought to curry favor with her by playing up her most flattering trait, that of generous provider of ice in a tropical land, the source of the pure glacial streams that coursed through the arid landscape like life-giving blood. On the other hand, perhaps what they meant was "ice queen," for she was also a treacherous seductress. She tormented the expedition of the great explorer Alexander von Humboldt with altitude sickness, forcing him and his crew to turn back. More than a century and a half later, she claimed the lives of 59 passengers of a flight that dared to skim her misty veil; the bodies were not discovered for another 26 years.

By the time we reached the refuge, conditions were approaching a complete whiteout. A guard offered me a steaming mug of tea and stamped my passport with a likeness of Chimborazo.

"Thanks," I said as I rubbed my thumb over the indigo ink. "Guess this is as close to seeing it as I am going to get."

The guard laughed. "You and everyone else. She tends to be very elusive."

We returned to Riobamba, and I wandered through streets clogged with buyers and sellers for the Saturday market. Clad in brilliantly hued ponchos—magenta, royal blue, fiery red, and forest green—and black bowler hats, some of highlanders were barefoot. Squatting around the fountains, huddling together on the park benches, and milling about on the streets, they spread their wares on the curb, beneath bright awnings, across rickety old wooden tables, and on hastily assembled wire racks. There were rows upon rows of colorful folk paintings depicting fat happy peasants toiling in lush green fields; char grilled guinea pigs bearing alarmed expressions; the ubiquitous woven purses and knapsacks, with their strange geometric designs; and towering pyramids of bananas and plantains.

A litter of squealing piglets brushed against my leg, led by their owner with a coarse rope. Up ahead, rows of vendors hawked fried pork and potatoes, a full-grown pig's head grinning from ear to ear displayed front and center at each stall. It was a sign that the meat was fresh and from a healthy, fat pig. I looked down at the piglets trailing past. I'd squeal if I were you too, I thought.

I met up with Jeannie and we headed for the bus station. A bus was just leaving for Quito, so we climbed aboard, accommodating ourselves in the only space left available—the cushion thrown on top of the motor, a gently vibrating trapezoidal rubber mound upon which passengers vied for fanny space. I wiggled my ass from side to side, hoping to nudge the woman next to me a little further to the side, but instead she shot me a contemptuous look and scooted even closer, spreading her legs and thrusting her hips in my direction. I sighed. Whether outside the classroom or in, I always seemed to be on the losing side.

About an hour outside the city, the sky began to darken. "Must be a snowstorm up in the mountains," I mused.

Jeannie shrugged and resumed reading her book, while I stared at the green and gold fields hugging the contours of the mountains like a velvet carpet. The cows, the goats, and the people making their way through the fields all wore the same docile expression. They looked passively at the bus as if to say, and where are you in such a hurry to get to? Having learned to be indifferent to that which they cannot control, they trundled resolutely through the fields, babies tied to the women's backs with colorful woven cloths, unconcerned with the blackness enveloping them.

The radio began to cackle. "*Volcán*," I heard an excited voice exclaim, and the word began to rumble through the bus, slowly building to a crescendo. It was northwest of Quito, they said. Or maybe just west. Or maybe it was even Rucu Pichincha on Quito's western flank, a tree-covered wall of rock that rose abruptly from the valley floor not one mile from the Center. The radio announcers couldn't agree which volcano had erupted, or which regions would be the most affected, or if there would be further eruptions. All we knew was that it was not a snowstorm.

It was all so surreal. I had imagined being held up at gunpoint. I had woken up in a cold sweat from dreams about being trapped in our downtown center, barricaded behind a wall of foosball tables, gunshots whistling through the air as the acrid smell of burning tires filled the courtyard. Once I had even convinced myself—as I lay on the bathroom floor in agony after eating some iridescent mystery meat—that I might have a tapeworm, and that any minute a three-foot long slimy organism might slither out of my nether regions, wrap itself around my leg, and start sucking out all of my blood. But somehow I had never envisioned being in a volcanic eruption. Which was strange, given that Ecuador has some of the most active volcanoes in the world.

The most unsettling part was that we were actually driving *into* the ash cloud. "Shouldn't we be driving away from it?" I wondered aloud. I couldn't remember any emergency situation in which you were supposed to go *towards* the threat. In a fire, you were supposed to stop, drop, and roll—away from the fire. If you heard a tornado siren, you were supposed to stay in the basement rather than go outside and chase the cyclone with your video camera. Everyone knew what happened to those people: they died.

But here we were, racing towards the disaster, full speed ahead. "I hope it isn't Rucu," Jeannie said. She looked shell-shocked and she chewed on two fingernails at once. I had never seen her so tense. "The whole center would probably be buried. Like Pompeii."

The dust on the trees grew thicker and thicker, their branches weighted down, bowing low to the ground. One-room mud brick homes with corrugated tin roofs began to dot the hillsides, and the road widened into several lanes. I could tell we were getting close to the city.

Traffic ground to a halt. Drivers merged, clogging already congested lanes, as the police closed several lanes of the freeway to allow for emergency vehicles. "Incredible," Jeannie murmured. "For once the police are actually making themselves useful."

With the visibility next to zero, we inched along. The passengers became silent and withdrawn; the only one moving at all seemed to be the driver's assistant, who periodically leapt off the bus clutching a plastic bucket, sprinkled the windshield with what little water we had left, and staggered back on board in a coughing fit.

The air inside grew thick and heavy. My throat stung. I could almost picture burning embers of ash searing my tonsils, my tongue, and my esophagus like a million cigarette burns. I stared forlornly at the inch of water left in my water bottle. Should I save it for later? No, I decided. I had to have relief now. Chugging it down, I swallowed hard, but relief was elusive. My tongue was so dry I could feel every ridge.

Outside, ash fell like snow, and the few people walking the streets wore surgical masks. As the radio announcer's deep, resonant voice expounded on the dangers of inhaling volcanic ash, exhorting his listeners to stay indoors, Jeannie and I improvised as best we could. I carefully folded my long underwear into a neat rectangle, placed the wad of soft cotton over my nose and mouth, and tied the sleeves into a tight knot at the nape of my neck. Jeannie slipped her bandana out of her backpack and secured it in place. As we stepped off the bus into the eerie quiet of the city, I felt like a masked guerilla descending from the sierra to mount an attack.

We caught a city bus and glided past shuttered shops and parked cars encrusted with a thick layer of ash. The bus stopped three blocks short of the center, and we began trekking through a steady rain of ash. It was hard to breathe, and the air smelled of sulfur. Gritty flecks clung to our eyelashes. At last, I spotted the center in the distance, emerging from the darkness like a shining white bulwark against Mother Nature.

"We're almost there!" I tried to shout to Jeannie, overjoyed. But it came out more as a whimper, muffled by a thick wad of cotton. I could taste my pajamas.

For once, the gate was open. We plodded through the ash, leaving behind us a trail of footprints that exposed the concrete parking lot beneath us. Around the back, I jiggled the key impatiently in the lock. One turn. Two turns. Then a gentle push, and we were inside. Jeannie slammed the door shut as quickly as possible and we unmasked ourselves, inhaling deeply. I laughed as I looked over at Jeannie, who was slumped against the door. She looked like a raccoon, her eyes ringed with ash, the lower portion of her face, which had been covered, smooth and pale.

We raced up the steps to the kitchen. Flinging my backpack on the floor, I grabbed a glass from the cabinet and shoved it under the spigot of one of the barrels of boiled water.

Paul wandered into the kitchen, a deep furrow in his brow. Leaning against the counter, he held his lower back as if he were in pain. "Maureen," he said, "the Madres wanted me to tell you...." He shifted his stance uncomfortably and cleared his throat. "Oscar was run over by a car today and died. I'm sorry."

It was incredible, unbelievable. And yet his expression told me that it was true. "I don't understand," I gasped. "He was just crossing the street and...?"

"No, he was selling candy on the bus. He did that too, you know, besides shining shoes...I guess he wasn't looking when he stepped off the bus in the middle of traffic and a speeding driver hit him. They took him to the hospital, but the doctors were all watching the soccer championships on TV and didn't attend to him right away. He died in the waiting room."

Paul staggered out of the room, a bit dazed. I slumped against the counter and tried to take in the news. Oscar was dead. He died in a waiting room because Ecuadorian doctors can't be bothered to operate in the middle of a *fútbol* game, especially when they might not get paid. He was hit stepping off a bus in the middle of four lanes of traffic because Ecuadorian bus drivers can't be bothered to pull over to the curb. Bus drivers don't pull over to the curb because—simply put—no one makes them. Oscar was on the bus because his family depended on his income for their support. They depended on his support because they were poor. They were poor because they were indigenous migrants from the countryside with no social support system, no education, no skills, and too many hungry mouths to feed. Now that Oscar was dead, they were even more likely than before to stay poor. Oscar's death was part of the cycle, a cycle that began long before I arrived and that would probably continue long after I left.

I could not shake the memories of all the times I had wished Oscar out of my class. At the end of those interminable October days, when I would sit catatonic, staring at the wall and wondering how many more times I would pry Oscar off the floor, intercept his fists flying in the direction of a classmate's face, retrieve the Bingo prizes he had stolen from me, or make him sit alone in the corner, with his back to the class, I had fantasized that he would be demoted to sixth grade, or even—dare I admit it—kicked out of the Center. I had never, however, imagined him disemboweled by a speeding car. It seemed horribly unfair. His was a young life yet to be molded, yet to be straightened out, and now neither he—nor we—would be able to effect that change. It was as if God had given up on him, or decided this was one experiment that had gone awry and needed to be terminated.

I dragged myself upstairs, flipped on the bathroom light, and took a long, hard look at myself in the mirror. My skin was gray from all the specks of ash sticking to it. "From dust we are created and to dust we shall return," I whispered as a salty tear streaked a trail through the gritty ash. I turned off the light, crawled into bed, and cried myself to sleep.

When I awoke, the world was silent and gray. I stood at the window and watched as the guards below struggled against the shape-shifting silvery powder. One minute it was rippling across the pavement in a shimmering mass of shallow dunes and valleys, the next it reinvented itself as a cratered lunar landscape, and in yet a third incarnation it sprang up in a swirling vortex. Undeterred, the guards kept sweeping.

I got into the shower and turned on the tap. Tepid water sprayed over me, sending a heavy black sludge down my back as it dislodged thick flakes of ash from my hair. How appropriate, I thought, as a seemingly endless stream of inky liquid swirled around my feet and gurgled down the drain. The water matches my mood. And yet somehow there was nothing cathartic about seeing it sucked down the drain. I got out of the shower feeling as dirty as I had before.

Downstairs, the dining room was eerily silent, save for the angry howl of the wind outside. Zach wandered through in his plaid flannel pajamas. "Didn't you hear?" he said. "Classes are cancelled the rest of the week for volcano clean-up."

"Oh," I mumbled. The truth was that classes were the last thing on my mind.

He put a hand on my shoulder and squeezed gently. "I'm sorry about Oscar," he said.

"Me too."

He shuffled into the TV room. I have been wrong, I thought, about many things. Zach wasn't just a frat boy. Oscar was not just a little hellion, but a troubled kid living on borrowed time. I could not just drop into a new culture, figure out why they would risk everything to come to America, and then leave again, untouched and unaffected. I could not just be an observer. I was now part of the story too.

I poured myself a glass of *tomate de árbol* juice and went to sit in the dining room by the big picture windows. *Tomate de árbol* was my favorite juice. Fluorescent orange and pleasantly tart, it had a thick, silky texture that slid right down one's throat. To me, it smelled faintly of mossy rainforests and damp grassy meadows, and it conjured up images of a bounteous Eden sprouting exotic sustenance at every turn. Today, though, it tasted wrong, all wrong. As I watched the flakes stream past and reflected on Oscar's untimely end, the earth seemed neither bountiful nor beneficent; it seemed cruel and capricious, hostile and violent. It did not seem like the place in which people sip *tomate de árbol* juice over leisurely breakfasts, but rather a place in which people slake their thirst with colorless, bitter liquids, or worse yet, go thirsty.

In search of signs of life, I went outside. Two little girls, maybe six or seven years old, were scratching out a hopscotch rectangle in the grit with a stick, oblivious to the staff's attempt to organize clean-up activities around them. Three boys took turns on the slide. Apparently their parents hadn't heard, or didn't care, that exposure to volcanic ash can lead to serious respiratory illnesses.

Juan and Jefferson ran up to me. "Did you hear about Oscar?" Juan said. "He died."

"I know. Isn't that sad?"

Juan shrugged. "He stole my backpack."

"Now he won't beat me up on the playground," Jefferson chimed in.

"Well that's true," I said. It sounded so lame, but I couldn't think of anything else to say. It *was* true. It was also sad. But I didn't think there was any way I could get Juan and Jefferson to see that.

"We're going to play soccer now. Want to come watch?"

"Maybe later."

I headed out of the compound and down the hill, past the wall that separated us from the light manufacturing facility next door, with its shards of green and white glass forming an endless jagged line, and past the block of unremarkable, middle-class shops. Smartly dressed young women in surgical masks swept the pavement briskly. The other side of the street was lined with pastel-colored, two-story homes with sloping tile roofs and huge flowering bushes artfully planted to obscure the heavy metal gates that surrounded the property. "Upper-middle-class homes," one of the second-year volunteers had explained to me. "You know they are more than middle class because they feature electronic security systems and garages. You know they are less than truly upper class because they don't have armed guards patrolling the property. They would if they could afford it, but they can't." A few more blocks down the street, I reached the modern asphalt highway that cut a curving swath through the valley. On the opposite side of the highway, just before the scrubby hills of the shantytowns, a country club complete with an enormous golf course hid behind a huge fence and a thicket of trees. From what little I could see, no one was golfing today.

I walked a block alongside the highway, then turned abruptly into a warren of tiny curving streets. Just a block from the middle-class neighborhood through which I had strolled, this area harbored a poor community in which several of our school's families lived. Once it had been a true shantytown, with dirt streets and squatters building on any available piece of land, no matter how precarious, but in the space of twenty years, the area had acquired a certain orderliness, with the city eventually agreeing to extend paved roads to the area, and the buildings becoming more permanent over time. Now stray dogs roamed the streets and watchful, shifty-eyed shopkeepers peered out from their concrete, airless boxes, lit only by the sunlight, anxious at the sight of a stranger walking their streets. Skinny chickens scratched at concrete patios. I stared down a bedraggled rooster, wondering if this was the one that woke me every morning at dawn.

Rounding the corner, I passed the center's back gate and continued past a stately historical archives building, crossed the street, and came to a beautiful faux-colonial yellow municipal building with a lush garden in front and two straight, tall palm trees. I passed the small military post behind it and was half-relieved, half-annoyed, to find that the volcano had not altered the young soldiers' routine. "*Mamacita!*" A skinny teenage boy whistled approvingly as his two sidekicks stopped sweeping long enough to give me the once-over. I rolled my eyes, and perhaps they too felt comforted that the old routine lived on.

At the next corner, a commercial avenue intersected the street. As usual, I turned here to pass the noisy open-air seafood restaurant, the spits of roasted guinea pig, the vendors spilling out onto the street with their strange spiny fruits. Inside, posters of the Virgin Mary alternated with tacked-up pictures of huge-breasted naked blonde calendar girls. Three blocks up, this thoroughfare dead-ended at a cute little square in front of a colonial-era church. Drunks congregated on the benches, but the roving ice-cream sellers and the schoolgirls, some in neat little uniforms so unlike my students' ragged attire, kept the square from seeming too seedy.

I was relieved to see that today the scene was refreshingly the same. Finally, I had left the stultifying stillness behind, the all-permeating sense of death that emanated from the ashes. I sat on a bench and closed my eyes, the sun warming my face as it at last peeked through the grayness. I heard the children squealing, the drunks mumbling, and the scritch-scratch of traditional dried grass brooms on paving stones. The square felt alive. *I finally felt alive.*

"*Profesora!*" someone shouted jubilantly in my ear.

I opened my eyes and saw a small child, maybe ten or twelve, clutching a wooden shoeshine kit filled with dirty rags and tarnished tins of shoe polish. His hands were stained mahogany and boot black, and smears of polish ran across his nose, his cheeks, and his grubby T-shirt. His jogging pants were ripped.

He frowned when I failed to respond. "What? You don't recognize me?"

"Of course I do..." I trailed off as I struggled to place the voice. It was familiar, and yet the face and the body were not. They seemed out of sync. Outside the classroom, it was all out of context. I tried to picture the kid in front of me sitting in a desk, with a notebook and a pencil, or maybe slugging another kid. Ah, slugging another kid...now that seemed familiar. Was it one of the triplets? No, he was far too small. It was... "Edison!" I finally shouted.

He broke into a wide grin and I tried to look as though I had recognized him all along. It was strange how small and vulnerable he looked, how dirty and wretched. He seemed so much bigger in class, and so much tougher.

"What are you doing here?" I asked.

"Working."

"I thought you worked as a mechanic."

"I do. But I also make money on the side shining shoes. Want a shoeshine?"

"Sure." I stuck out my foot and he went to work. "Did you hear about Oscar?"

"Yeah."

"How do you feel about that?" I asked gently, hoping against hope that he would say something more charitable than Juan and Jefferson had.

Edison shrugged. "He owes me money and now I'll never get it back."

I sighed. Practicality had once more won out over sentimentality. That was just the way it was, and I would have to get used to it.

When he finished, I took out a quarter, the standard fee, and placed it in the wooden box. He took it out and placed it back in my hand.

"For you," he said, "it's free."

That evening, I strategically seated myself at the far dining room table with Madre Kathy, Madre Josefina, Padre José, and Hermano Paco. As usual Padre José said nothing, Madre Josefina chattered at Padre José in Spanish (spoken for the benefit of Hermano Paco, who didn't speak a word of English) in her flat American accent, and Madre Kathy was all business, interjecting comments about broken washing machines and truant students. I found the dynamic between the three of them fascinating. Madre Josefina and Padre José were like an old married couple, while Madre Kathy was always businesslike. Unbeknownst to them, Madre Josefina and Padre José had generated quite a bit of gossip over the years. "I don't know about that," I said to one of the laundresses when she leaned in conspiratorially and informed me that Madre and Padre were an item. "I live with them and I've never seen anything to suggest that." She cocked an eyebrow and clucked at my naiveté. "Well maybe not *now*," she said. "Maybe they are too old for that kind of exertion. But when they were younger, definitely. A man and a woman, living together in a big house...why, it's only natural!"

Natural, perhaps, but unlikely. Madre Josefina seemed far too pious and ladylike for such a thing, and Padre José seemed far too distant and uncommunicative. To me, he was an enigma, an odd cross between a saintly, contemplative ascetic and a rogue. On the one hand, he rarely spoke, ate little, rose every morning at four to say a private mass for the Madres, and had dedicated forty years of his life to serving the poor under very difficult circumstances. But on the few occasions he actually did speak, his razor-sharp wit and bracing cynicism dispelled all images of Padre as a hair shirt-wearing John the Baptist. Once, on a trip downtown, Madre Kathy recounted the day she told Padre that, after several years as a Peace Corps volunteer at the Center, she had decided to enter the convent. "All he said was 'Why you stubborn little bitch. It took you this long to figure it out?'" Madre Kathy laughed. "That's it. He didn't say another word for hours."

Hermano Paco seemed oblivious to these dynamics, however. He spent the dinner hour talking to, or about, his food, and tonight was no exception. "*Banana,*" he said in a loud voice, staring at the fruit, "*te voy a comer.*" He reverently peeled it, all the while singing its praises, and finally took a bite with an almost spiritual look on his face. "*Mmmm, qué bueno!*" he exclaimed, rubbing his belly and shaking his shiny black hair, cut in a bowl in the style of a medieval monk.

He turned to me and smiled. "*Me gusta la fruta,*" he explained as if I hadn't just witnessed his paean to the noble banana, or his homage to a ripe mango the day before, or his peals of delight over the pulpy green *chirimoya* the day before that. Then he plunged into the soup with gusto, praising the digestive properties of chicken broth and thanking the little green peas for being so plump and juicy.

When there was a lull in the conversation, I asked about Oscar's family. "It's too bad about Oscar," Padre José said. "It's really a shame for the family. He was their oldest boy, a good source of income, you know? This is going to be hard on them financially."

I resented Padre's tone. It cheapened Oscar's death somehow; it reduced him to a mere income stream, and a measly one at that. But I was in no mood to argue with Padre; I just wanted information. "When is the funeral?"

Padre shrugged and rubbed the corner of his eye. "Don't know if there'll be one. I'm afraid the family may have fallen under the sway of some of those damn Jehovah's witnesses. They have some pretty weird ideas, you know, like insisting that you bury the dead on the day of death without a proper funeral or anything. Sometimes they just stick people in the ground in cardboard boxes."

"But isn't that a good thing?"

"What do you mean?"

"Well, poor Ecuadorians don't embalm or otherwise preserve the dead before burial. So it seems like a quick burial is more sanitary."

Padre peered over his glasses at me. "It's not a proper Christian burial."

And that was that. From there the conversation veered right back to extolling the virtues of carrots and debating the merits of a new purchase for the library.

I excused myself from the table and went to my room. Curled up on my bed, Padre's comment about the financial hardship imposed by Oscar's death echoed through my head. Life is so cheap here, I thought. Maybe it has to be. So many people die so often that you could go crazy if you thought too much about it.

I lay awake for hours, struggling to persuade myself of this. But even as the first rays of light penetrated my room, I remained unconvinced, plagued by the sneaking suspicion that if life weren't so cheap, a whole lot less people would die.

CHAPTER FOUR

Before long it became woefully apparent that something needed to be done about my *nivelación* boys. Even Juan, who seemed to have taken stock of the situation and realized he was one of the bigger boys, had begun misbehaving. My earlier confidence had dissipated entirely, and I was open to suggestions from all quarters.

"Reward the well-behaved kids with a game of Bingo on Friday," Sister Marlene, a visiting ninety-year-old nun who had taught at the center twenty years ago, advised.

"We already play Division Bingo every Friday. You know, I called out eighty-one divided by nine, and they put a marker on nine…"

"Yeah, I know. And?"

"Even the good kids try to steal the Bingo prizes. I have to resort to walking around the room with the bag of suckers clutched to my chest at all times. And they cheat and steal each other's winning cards."

She clucked disapprovingly. "That never happened to me."

"Talk to their parents at parent-teacher conference night," Madre Josefina counseled. So I joined the other volunteers on stage for introductions, concluding my brief remarks—delivered in self-consciously rapid-fire Spanish to allay the concerns of parents mystified by exactly why a *gringa* was teaching their children Spanish—with a special plea to meet with *nivelación* parents one-on-one to discuss their sons' bad behavior.

I squeezed through the crowd to grab a glass of *colada morada*. I was just gulping down a glass of the peculiar beverage—a substance rather like hot, thickened blueberry juice—when Jeannie came up behind me. "Psst. All the parents already forgot your name, so you know what they are calling you? '*La flaquita que habla como una española.*' The skinny one who talks like a Spaniard."

"Great." Not that they were wrong. I did have something of a Spanish accent, and I was *flaquita*. Seventeen pounds and three months ago people had described me as "slender"; now I could feel my ribs poking into my mattress at night. Sometimes I caught a glimpse of myself in a store window and didn't even recognize myself.

I backed away from the table and squeezed through the crowd. At the back of the room, families sat at long, narrow cafeteria tables sipping *colada morada* and nibbling cookies. The parents looked frightened and out of place, bewildered by their loud, brash, citified children. It was a shock to realize that many of these couples, despite their sagging skin and missing teeth, were about my age; most of the women had had their first child at fourteen or fifteen, and ten years and several children later, they looked old.

They wore indigenous costumes—embroidered white blouses, dark felt skirts, and a colorful sash—with matching fat, black braids snaking down their backs, some flecked with gray. Their husbands were short and squat, with thick necks, and wore old trousers and mismatched shirts, most likely hand-me-downs from American benefactors. A few even wore telltale Packers jerseys and "I love Milwaukee" T-shirts; Madre Josefina's sister lived in Milwaukee and directed most of the volunteer and donor outreach.

I spotted little Jefferson with a tiny couple, ostensibly his parents, and went over to speak to them. They looked very surprised for a moment, then stared assiduously at their feet.

"*Hola, Jefferson,*" I boomed as if they were all deaf.

"*Hola, Maureen,*" my little Muppet replied cheerily. "These are my parents." With that introduction, he ran off to play.

"Señor y Señora Martínez, I wanted to talk to you about Jefferson' behavior." They were still looking at their feet. I too looked down at their feet, suddenly afraid I might be stepping on them. I was relieved to see just two pairs of very old, very scuffed up shoes. I crouched lower, until I was almost kneeling on the floor, trying to meet their downcast gaze. I started the discussion with a frank acknowledgement of his lack of interest in learning.

"Oh, teacher," Señora Martínez murmured, now staring at my kneecaps. She addressed me in the most servile of manners, as if I were granting her an enormous favor just by deigning to speak with her. She rocked back and forth slowly. "Jefferson has always been slow, he was dropped on his head as a baby." She warmed to her lament. "We are humble people. We don't have an education. I am slow. They tried to teach me to read, but it is impossible. I'm just a washerwoman." Señor Martínez nodded along.

"It's not that Jefferson is slow, Señora. The problem is he doesn't do his homework. He doesn't do the worksheets I assign in class. He doesn't pay attention and he doesn't listen to me. He throws spitballs and gets into fights instead."

The couple abruptly stopped rocking and nodding. "Doesn't do his work?" Señor Martínez snapped, finally looking up.

"Right. I tell him to—"

"He disrespects you?"

"Well, yes, he—"

"The next time he gives you any trouble, just smack him across the face." Señor Martínez raised his hand and struck an imaginary object, hard. "Then you won't have any more problems with him. And be sure to let us know. We'll give him a good beating at home."

I was stunned. In the States you could get slapped with a lawsuit for hugging a kid, and these parents wanted me to *hit* their kid? And not just a slap on the wrist, but a bruising blow to the face. Didn't they realize that even after all of my weight loss I was still *twice* their son's size? And still part of me was not that surprised; it explained quite a lot of things: why Jefferson seemed to flinch involuntarily every time I raised my hand in a mock threat, why he never felt the need to obey me. I just wasn't very scary compared with his dad.

"I use my *cinturón*," Señor Martínez offered, his eyes gleaming. I tried to picture the delicate-looking man in front of me striking Jefferson with his belt. In my mind, the belt was black and frayed at the edges. It had a few extra holes crudely cut into it to accommodate Señor Martínez's girlish waist, which couldn't have been more than twenty-four inches in circumference, and a broken buckle dangling from the end. And there was that same gleam in his eyes. What *was* that? Cruel enjoyment? Power? Control? Or could it even be pride? Did he think that his emphasis on "discipline" made him a good father?

"You can borrow it if you want," he offered.

"*No, gracias,*" I mumbled. Out of the corner of my eye, I spied Jefferson playing marbles with another boy and felt a sudden rush of affection towards him. Poor kid. "I have another family I must go speak with," I said abruptly and hurried off.

"Remember," Señor Martínez shouted after me, "my *cinturón* is always at your disposal."

As I made my way from family to family, the Martínez' response was nearly universal. The mother of one of my students advocated biting. "Not enough to draw blood," she instructed me as she handed her youngest some construction paper and a pink crayon. "But hard enough to leave a mark."

Another shared a different technique. "Yank him out of his seat by his ear," she said. "That will show him who's boss." Evidently she had used this technique, and others, often: open sores festered on each of her children's earlobes, and scabs covered vast swathes of the youngest child's face.

I scanned the cafeteria anxiously as she chattered on about the merits of using one fist or two, a closed fist or an open palm. In one corner, Madre Josefina was wagging a finger in a portly woman's face. In another, Padre José and Madre Kathy were hunkered down in earnest conversation, while a few feet away Jeannie was leading a cadre of eager first-graders in a spirited rendition of the Hokey Pokey. Every now and then, my interlocutor poked me in the arm and asked if I was paying attention to her tips. Each time, I managed to mumble something and she seemed placated.

At last my eyes alighted on Señor Echeverría. Seated at a long table in the corner, he beamed with pride as he bounced his baby daughter on his knee. One of the few literate parents in the Center, he attended Mass regularly, was affectionate with his children and friendly with the volunteers, and had raised four studious, relatively well-behaved children. Padre and the Madres considered the family a model for others and had even recruited Señor Echeverría to be one of the Center's "leaders."

"Excuse me," I said. "There's another family I must speak with.'

I squeezed my way through the crowd, and a palpable sense of relief came over me as his four healthy children came into view, with their freshly laundered clothes and shampoo-shiny hair. No mucus, no urine stains, no scabs. All earlobes were intact.

"Señor Echeverría," I greeted him warmly.

"Señorita Maureen." He looked me in the eye and smiled.

I congratulated him on his new daughter and informed him that his oldest daughter was doing very well in my Spanish class. "Your son, however,"—I looked over at his son, who squirmed and dashed off—"has been giving me problems."

Señor Echeverría stiffened. His knee came to a sudden standstill, and the baby shifted uneasily in her pink ruffled dress, her rosy lips curling into a pout. She looked like she wanted to cry, but was afraid to. "I am very sorry to hear that," he said in a grave voice.

"Will you speak to him about his behavior?"

"Better than that," he assured me. "Tonight I will be sure to give him a beating he won't soon forget. You can be sure he won't give you any more trouble after that."

I sighed weakly, and he grasped my hand firmly and beamed up at me, thrilled that he could be of service. "I'm so glad we had this talk," he said. "Please let me know if there is anything more I can do."

As he contentedly resumed bouncing his daughter and the toothy grin returned to her face, I suddenly felt very tired. Slipping back into the crowd, I made my way to the soccer field. There, in the stillness of the evening, I slumped against a pillar and sucked in deep breaths of cool mountain air. Sliding down into the damp earth, I lay down in the grit and looked up at the stars. Somewhere out there, I told myself, is an Ecuadorian family that doesn't beat their kids. I just don't know them.

Two girls came running out onto the field. "Marcia!" a raven-haired girl in a blue dress shrieked in delight as she chased after her older companion. Piercing the night with their shrieks and peals of laughter, they crisscrossed the field in great looping circles. The younger girl's ruby red heels glinted in the moonlight as she wobbled in gleeful pursuit.

I was envious. I wanted to be that happy, that carefree. I wanted to live in the moment, not obsess over what happened yesterday or worry about what would happen tomorrow. Not worry about what happened to Jefferson or Edison when they went home at night. *I* wanted ruby red slippers. I wanted to click them three times together and be magically transported home or, if not home, at least to a place far less complicated.

I stretched out my legs. Bagged around my knees, my Ecuadorian jeans ended an unflattering couple of inches above my ankle. A pink, fleshy big toe poked out of my right tennis shoe.

I closed my eyes and tapped my toes together. One. The shrieking continued. Two. A thud, then a peal of laughter. Three. Silence.

When at last I opened my eyes, the girls were gone. But I was still lying on an Ecuadorian soccer field, still caked in dirt, and still wondering when, if ever, the cycle of violence would end.

Don Rodrigo, the Inspector, and Madre Kathy soon wearied of the revolving door of miscreants I sent their way. I got tired of sending them. A trip to the Inspector seemed to be good for fifteen minutes' of improved behavior, a trip to Don Rodrigo for one class, and a trip to Madre Kathy two or three classes, although with the drawback that the child in question hated me when I let them back into class after a talk with Madre Kathy. "What does she say to them? Why is she so effective?" I asked the Inspector.

"She tells them they aren't going to eat that day."

"Oh." No wonder they had such long faces.

One typically hellish afternoon someone pinched my ass as I leaned over to intervene in a fistfight. I spun around in a fury. If I didn't demand respect now, my chances of ever getting it were gone forever. "WHO DID THAT?"

Four sets of beady eyes gazed at me blankly. They were counting on my sense of justice to get the better of me; they expected that since I couldn't say for sure who the culprit was, no one would be punished. I hesitated for a moment, trying to divine who seemed guilty. One of the triplets looked down for a second.

"YOU!" I thundered, waving a finger in his face. "You are coming with me!" I yanked him out of his seat and marched him down the hall to the Inspector's office. "He pinched my ass!" I screamed at the Inspector, as if it was his fault. "He CANNOT come back to my class! Never. Ever. No matter what the Madre says. I will quit. He can. Never. Set. Foot. In. My. Classroom. Again."

The Inspector did not argue with me. He railed at the reputed offender and then personally escorted him to Madre Kathy. I stomped back to class and slammed the door with such force it almost came off its hinges. Most of the kids actually jumped in their seats. It was absolutely silent. I opened the door and slammed it again for good effect. Then I stared each and every one of them down as I paced up and down the aisles like a caged tiger. "I have had it with all of you!" I shouted. "Do you know what it is like to travel four thousand miles, to come to a new country, to be away from your family and friends, to work for FREE, and then to have to put up with you? I cannot believe the lack of respect you show for someone who is trying hard to teach you, to guide you, to improve your life!" I pointed accusatorily at Juan. "You! Do want to be poor and miserable your whole life?"

"N-no," he stammered.

"Is this what God wants for you?" I demanded.

"N-no, I don't think so."

"Doesn't the Center give you three meals a day?"

"*Sí, profesora.*"

"And free medical care?"

"*Sí, profesora.*"

"And free job training? And free clothing? And sacks of rice and beans for your family at Christmas?"

"*Sí, profesora, sí.*"

"And is this how you show your gratitude?"

They looked at me wide-eyed and terrified.

"IS IT?" A few timidly shook their heads no. "Good. Then consider yourselves warned. Tomorrow a whole new regime begins. Anyone not with the program is going to be out on the street and I don't give a damn if you starve to death or end up in prison or die a horrible death from hepatitis." I swung open the door and let it bang against the wall for dramatic effect. "Class dismissed."

For the first time all year, they filed out for their five-minute break in silence. I went to the Inspector's office to fill out the daily attendance and behavior report and leaned over the book, shaking with anger and frustration. "Miguel pinched my ass," I wrote. I bet Madre Kathy didn't read that every day. "He can never, ever come back to my class," I added, underlining each word three times. "Franklin hit Jefferson, Darwin tried to steal chalk, and Juan arrived fifteen minutes late."

I was contemplating whether I should write more when the Inspector and an Ecuadorian teacher walked into the room. "You need to learn to control your class, Maureen," the Inspector said in an irritated voice.

I couldn't believe it. "*I* am doing the best I can. *They* are little monsters. *They* kick each other and fight and throw spitballs and no matter how much I yell or send them to you or Don Rodrigo or Madre Kathy nothing changes! Why don't YOU or Don Rodrigo or Madre Kathy DO SOMETHING? I wasn't trained for this. I'm not really a teacher. I—"

Tears welled up in my eyes. If I said another word, I would start crying like a baby. It was all too humiliating, being bested by some immature hormonal midgets, sexually harassed by a fifteen-year-old, not even getting paid for the whole ordeal, and then not receiving even one iota of support or sympathy from people who ought to understand, if not downright appreciate me for my willingness to do a thankless job for free.

"Calm down, calm down," the teacher said impatiently, but with a twinge of sympathy. "I'll tell you what you should do. Give them some physical chore to do. It'll be more effective than yelling yourself hoarse."

I thanked her and ran out of the room.

The next day I introduced my wayward boys to the concept of bathroom duty. "The first time I write your name on the chalkboard, consider it a warning. After that, every time you misbehave I put a checkmark next to your name. At the end of the week, I count up the checkmarks and each one counts as half an hour of bathroom duty. That weekend you will clean the boys' bathroom for the specified number of hours. Any questions?"

Juan looked defeated for a moment, then lit up. "But Maureen, we all work on Saturdays so there is no way we can come and scrub the bathroom."

"What time do you work on Saturdays?"

"Five a.m."

"Now that is a lie," I said triumphantly. My kids were champion fibbers, with some of the best poker faces I had ever seen, the most creative tall tales, and the most irresistible puppy-dog brown eyes. But today I had outsmarted them; I had done my homework beforehand. "Madre Kathy says no one starts before eight. If you work at eight, I'll see you at seven. And if you have more than a half hour of duty, I'll see you at six or five or four—"

Jefferson snickered. "But then you'll have to get out of bed with Paaaaaaablo."

"Ooooooh, Paaaaaaaablo," Juan and Wilson, a pudgy, normally quiet boy, cooed like Motown back-up singers.

I sighed. All of this incessant ribbing about 'Pablo' was getting old. Sometimes I felt like I was teaching class to a bunch of paparazzi. I walked to the back of the classroom and placed one hand on Jefferson's shoulder and the other on Wilson's. I clamped down with a bit of pressure to show I meant business. "Forget about Pablo. I will always make time for you guys. Whether to teach you, or to punish you. And that is a promise."

I walked to the front of the classroom and commenced the lesson. Within a few minutes, Juan kicked Raúl's chair. I wrote his name on the board.

"But Maureen, I didn't do anything. I was just sitting here and his chair just moved all of the sudden."

"*BAÑOS!*" I roared with glee as I checked off his name.

"What did I do?"

"You lied."

"No, I didn't. I just—"

"Oh, you lied again! Another half hour!"

"But I—"

"Careful, Juan. You want to go for an hour and a half? We could do that. It takes a while to scrub the floors and the showers and the toilets and the urinals."

Raúl screwed up his face. "Urinals? That's disgusting, Maureen."

"Then don't misbehave." I turned back to Juan. "So? Want another half hour?"

He gritted his teeth. "No."

On Sunday afternoon, Juan arrived at the back gate looking somewhat chastened without his adoring posse. I met him with a pail, a bottle of toilet bowl cleaner, a scrub brush, some soap, and a few rags. "Hope you're ready to work," I chirped. "The bathroom's pretty gross."

I led him to the upstairs bathroom and into a stall. It reeked and the toilet hadn't been flushed in a few days. The floor was stained with urine and streaked with rivulets of dirty water. There was no toilet paper to be found anywhere—the center didn't stock it. "No one uses it anyway," Madre Kathy had explained.

I showed him how to flush the toilet, then squeeze disinfectant into the bowl, let it sit for a moment, and scrub under the rim and flush again. Having been forbidden by Madre Kathy to leave Juan unattended for even a minute, lest he wreak havoc on the bathroom, I had no choice but to drag a bench into the bathroom and supervise. I inched the bench closer to the fresh air coming through the door and pulled out a dog-eared copy of *War and Peace*, hoping to take my mind off the nauseating stench that permeated every corner of the room.

A few minutes later Juan was standing before me, scrub brush in hand. "Okay, I finished the toilets," he said, and I went to inspect his handiwork. To my surprise, he had actually done a good job. "Now the urinals," I instructed. "Inside and out."

He took to his task with great industriousness, following the curve of the porcelain with his brush and then gently scrubbing the inside lip. It's just like he's shining shoes, I thought. "What's it like to ride a plane?" Juan asked.

"Weird," I said, struggling to remember what it was like to be on a plane for the first time. It had been so long ago, and in the interim I had been on dozens of planes, eaten countless packets of pretzels, flown through thousands of clouds and buzzed over hundreds of shimmering lakes. The exotic had become routine, even boring. But he looked at me expectantly, and I knew he wanted something more from me. I sensed that he wanted me to say something magical, fantastic. "Well," I finally said, "the houses below look like little tiny boxes and the cars look like ants."

"What do people look like?"

"They're so small you can't even see them."

"Really?" He looked very impressed.

"Really."

"Do you go upside down?"

"No," I said and he looked disappointed. I think he had seen a bootlegged copy of *Top Gun* a few too many times. "But," I added, "sometimes you go sideways and you get dizzy."

"Do you throw up all over people?"

"Not usually." But then I remembered how I used to hover over the little white barf bags when I was little, with my sister futilely pressing the pressure points on my wrist. "But some people do. I used to."

"Have you ever crash landed in the jungle?"

"Do I look like I've ever crash landed in the jungle?"

"I don't know."

"If someone crash lands, they're pretty much dead, Juan. And if they're not, they will have cracked ribs and all kinds of problems."

"Oh."

"You go on top of the clouds, though."

"*Chévere*," he said. It was the all-purpose Ecuadorian word for "cool."

We talked about life in America, and the Madres and the Padre (he had heard Madre Josefina and Padre José were an item too—apparently it was a popular rumor), and the other volunteers (Katherine was the most *bonita*, according to his poll of the junior high boys), and sports, especially soccer.

"Who's your favorite soccer team?" he demanded to know.

"Uh...." I stammered. A minute ago I had been *chévere*—or at the very least I had done something *chévere*, which I decided was close enough to the same thing—and now I was on the verge of admitting I didn't even know the name of the Ecuadorian soccer teams. Wait a minute, I thought, last week Jeannie went to a soccer game—complete with fans throwing burning items on the field and all—and the name was... "*Liga!*" I said suddenly and just a tad too loudly.

He eyed me suspiciously. "They're okay, I suppose."

"I went to my first bullfight yesterday," I volunteered. What I didn't say was that it was probably also my last. There was something so unfair, so unsportsmanlike about it. The matador didn't even get near the bull until the bull had at least five daggers sticking in it, and then the matador pranced around in his sissy tights, taunting the poor bull while a few thousand spectators sat in the searing sun and watched the bull's blood slowly seep into the reddish-brown earth. It was somewhat nauseating, and definitely weird. Not what I would call proper entertainment.

"Was there lots of blood?" he asked excitedly.

I nodded weakly.

"How much did it cost?"

"It was a little on the expensive side," I said, embarrassed.

"How much?"

"Fifteen dollars," I said in a small voice. Fifteen dollars was as much as he would earn in a week.

"If you have so much money, you should give some to me." It was hard to argue with that kind of logic.

An hour later, I told him he was free to go. To my surprise, he actually looked a little disappointed. I gave him the standard speech about hard work, discipline, and preparing for a better future. He seemed to take it to heart. We shook hands, and I noticed his strong grip. He would be a man soon and that much harder to control. This was a closing window of opportunity; in a few years, he'd either be a strapping, ambitious young man or a terrific thug. He could go either way.

And so it was that I became a weekend fixture in the men's room. No one seemed to feel the slightest embarrassment. "*Hola, Maureen!*" teenagers that I had never met would yell as they raced to the urinals. And every time, even though I sat on the other side of the partition, where the sinks were, I would still feel the need to avert my eyes.

And every time, just like that first day with Juan, I passed the time listening to my students' stories or answering their questions. A lot of the stories were funny, but some were heartbreaking, like the day Raúl told me his family had to come up with ten dollars in a hurry to pay for a prescription for his ailing grandmother. "What will happen if she doesn't get the medicine in time?"

He shrugged. "Oh, she'll die, I guess."

"I could just give your family the ten dollars."

He looked offended. "Don't worry. My dad said he'll work extra shifts all week and he'll come up with the money. If he says so, he will."

Behavior steadily improved.

CHAPTER FIVE

In November, our TV was hijacked. The peppy commercials featuring white Hispanic families (who looked nothing like the people we actually knew) waxing poetic on the benefits of dairy and canned peas became fewer and farther between. In their place were ads featuring a fat, balding, middle-aged man with an idiotic smile plastered on his face. At the end of each commercial he pumped his arms ecstatically. Ostensibly a victory salute, to us gringos it looked like Spasimodo giving a Nazi salute.

"Who is that moron?" I mused absentmindedly as I bled red ink over the latest round of spelling tests.

"Álvaro Noboa," Jeannie said, as if this was obvious. "He's the frontrunner for the presidency."

"He looks like a used car salesman in a second-rate Texas border town."

"Actually he's the richest man in Ecuador."

"Really?"

"Yup. He made a fortune on bananas. And he has a monopoly on the entire Ecuadorian market for flour. He raised the price of flour twenty-five percent last week, but no one in the media seems to care."

That much, at least, was not a surprise. The Ecuadorian papers were filled with numerous arcane political squabbles and fallings-out, but little of real substance. There were always at least three typos on the front page, and the news was mind-numbingly boring and irrelevant. As a result, the Padre and the Madres also subscribed to the *Miami Herald*, which, while not exactly the *New*

York Times, seemed to have more substantive coverage of Ecuadorian politics than the Ecuadorian papers.

Embarrassed by my ignorance of the upcoming election, I began reading the papers religiously. What I soon discovered was that the Ecuadorian papers, in the main, were squarely in the Noboa camp. They splashed photos of him distributing refrigerators to his supporters at campaign stops across the front page and hinted that his primary opponent, the handsome Lucio Gutiérrez, was a Marxist firebrand in the mold of Hugo Chávez. They published fawning fluff pieces about the candidates' wives and reported that Noboa spent yet another day resting in one of his many villas, exhausted from the strain of campaigning. One wondered how he'd fare with the strain of actually governing.

English-language press outlets were far less sanguine about the country's choices. Human Rights Watch reported that children as young as eight years old worked 12-hour days in the Noboa Group's supplier plantations, forced to perform dangerous work using sharp knives and machetes, and suffered rashes and intestinal illnesses stemming from direct exposure to toxic pesticides. The *New York Times* reported that masked gunmen attacked striking workers on these same plantations, wounding two.

Colonel Gutiérrez—known as "Lucio" to the adoring masses—had a checkered history of his own. A relatively obscure army colonel throughout the 1990s, he rose to national prominence in January 2000 during massive demonstrations by indigenous peasants outraged by then-President Jamil Mahuad's adoption of neo-liberal economic policies. Ordered by his commanding officer to disperse the angry mob, Colonel Gutiérrez instead set up mobile army kitchens to feed the protesters and stood by as they occupied the nation's Congress building. The resulting government of "national salvation" did not last long. The old regime was returned to power, albeit with the vice-president succeeding the now discredited Mahuad, and Colonel Gutiérrez was imprisoned and stripped of his military title. Released to much fanfare six months later, the charismatic Gutiérrez restyled himself as Lucio, Man of the People, and launched a political career culminating in his underdog campaign against Noboa.

Given this history, one might suppose that the Ecuadorian press would have been concerned about his commitment to democracy. Not so. They contented themselves to rail against his left-leaning economic proposals, leaving *The Miami Herald*'s editorial page to sound the alarm bells.

Wondering what the Madres and Padre's take was, I followed them into the library after dinner one evening. Padre crossed one gaunt leg over the other and peered over his glasses at me. Madre Josefina cocked an eyebrow in my direction. They didn't try to conceal their surprise: it was exceedingly rare for me to seek them out. "So," I said casually, as if I were just making idle chit-chat, "Who do you want to win?"

"Well he won't win, but I guess I would prefer Rodrigo Borja." Padre pushed his glasses up the bridge of his nose and grimaced. Madre murmured her assent.

"Why? Is he less corrupt that the others?"

"No, probably not. But at least he's the devil we know, as opposed to the devil we don't know. He already was president, you see, some years ago. He was corrupt, but at least we know how corrupt to expect him to be. And the economy ran reasonably well. He managed what he and his cronies didn't steal pretty well."

Now there, I thought, was a campaign slogan one didn't hear often: He's a crook, but he's a smart crook.

"It's doesn't really matter what we think, though," Madre said. She smoothed her dress over her knee. She looked resigned, but also serene. She seemed to have made her peace with all of this a long time ago. "We're not citizens so we can't vote."

"Have you ever thought of becoming citizens? So you could vote?"

Madre laughed. "Why would we want to do that? It's all one big joke. We had one president, Abdalá Bucaram, who used to arrive at his public appearances in a helicopter and then run out dressed as Batman. He thought he was a superhero."

Padre grimaced. "He also lunched with Lorena Bobbitt and recorded a pop song."

"Of course, Bucaram's in exile now in Panama. Took the whole contents of the Presidential Palace with him when he left, plus millions of dollars stuffed in suitcases. They say he's preparing a comeback, though." She shrugged. "So you see, nothing ever really changes. Voting is pointless."

Their indifference rankled me a bit, and yet I had to admit that I didn't have a clear idea of who the best candidate was either. In a campaign with only the vaguest of policy platforms and no debates, it all came down to character and experience. And in that regard, it was not encouraging. The only two viable candidates seemed to be a corrupt fat cat who exploited the workers on his plantations and exercised his monopoly over the entire Ecuadorian flour market to raise the price of this poor people's staple astronomically (during the campaign, no less), and a former leftist coup leader who could very well lead the country into class warfare, an economic free fall, and international pariah status.

So for the sake of enlightenment, I polled my ninth grade Spanish class. Lucio came out ahead by a small margin.

"Why Lucio?"

Silvia, one of the prettiest and most popular girls in the class, raised her hand. "I feel that he represents us and understands our needs because he is also from a poor background. But even though he is from that background, he rose to become a colonel and he did a good deed by ridding us of a corrupt administration."

"By force."

She looked confused.

"Doesn't anyone think that his willingness to overthrow a democratically elected government might mean that he is not as committed as he should be to democracy and the rule of law?" I asked, a tinge of desperation in my voice. Surely someone was bothered by this.

Thirty completely blank faces looked up at me. I guess not.

"And what about those that voted for Noboa? Why Noboa?"

A shaggy-haired boy who normally sat in the back of the room, sullen and withdrawn, shouted out an answer. "Isn't it obvious? He has so much money he doesn't need to steal it from us."

Several heads nodded in agreement. "He promised my mom a job in one of his factories if she votes for him," added one of my quieter girls. She folded her hands neatly on her desk and looked at me expectantly as if *now* I would understand why Noboa was such a great, shining beacon of hope.

"Isn't that corruption, though," I railed, "just as much as stealing money? Isn't trading favors corruption too?"

My kids shook their heads. No. And in that simple gesture I grasped an enduring truth: whatever they may tell pollsters and whatever they may chant at protests, voters don't dislike corruption. What they dislike is corruption that doesn't benefit them.

Much to the Padre and Madres' dismay, the government decreed that our center would serve as a polling station. "We'll just have to make the best of it," Madre Josefina said. "And watch those soldiers like a hawk. They're worse than the random voters who will be tramping through the place. Goodness knows what they will try to walk off with."

"Whatever you do, don't take any pictures," Madre Kathy warned. "It is strictly prohibited and if they catch you, the soldiers will go ballistic."

Determined to avoid tussles with these apparently hypersensitive, kleptomaniac conscripts, I resolved to stay barricaded in my room—or perhaps safely ensconced in a museum—during the two-day election weekend. A glimpse of a cadre of machine gun-toting soldiers taking up sniper positions on the junior high's second story reinforced my resolve for the first few hours, but as the crowd began to grow, it began to waver.

From the dining room windows, I watched as indigenous hordes poured out of the buses that whizzed by our front door while a few well-to-do voters arrived in SUVs, the windows tinted black. It was the only time all year I had seen large numbers of the indigent and the fabulously wealthy in close physical proximity. Compulsory voting was apparently the one greater leveler of Ecuadorian society: everyone, rich or poor, white or indigenous, politically active or completely apathetic, had to vote in order to be able to work, send their children to public school, receive government benefits, or do anything else remotely related to the functioning (or malfunctioning) of the government.

"It is just unbelievable out there, Maureen," Zach yelled as he ran through the dining room. "We've sold hundreds of servings of fried pork and potatoes to the folks in line. The restaurant has sold as much this lunch shift as they normally sell in a week."

I decided to investigate for myself.

Outside, the scene was ever more surreal than I had imagined. In the space of just a few hours, the crowd had worn a deep rut into our field. Across it marched a steady stream of dark-skinned peasants in billowing mud-spattered skirts, the various members of their brood strapped to their backs, balanced on their hips, and clinging to their skirts. Copious amounts of litter swirled about like urban tumbleweed. Drums beat, horns blared, and blasts of Shakira alternated with Andean pan pipes.

I didn't get far before I reached the end of the line. Snaking around the dirt soccer field, through the corridor, and into the bowels of the junior high, it was completely devoid of the almost funereal solemnity of American polling stations. Exuberance and chaos were the order of the day.

At the top of the first flight of stairs, I found Madre Josefina valiantly attempting to hold a couple of soldiers at bay. "*Prohibido! Prohibido!*" she shrieked, gesticulating wildly at the second flight of stairs, which was blocked with a table. Bemused, they shrugged and sauntered off down the corridor, machine guns tossed casually over their shoulder. The voters paid them no attention.

From my unobtrusive perch in the corner, I watched as each voter was handed a piece of paper and a pen. The official instructed him or her to stand behind a cardboard box and indicate his or her preferred candidate with an "X". The ballot had both the candidates' names and their supposedly identifying symbols to theoretically ensure that even illiterate voters—the majority of Ecuador's population—could vote.

That theory hadn't seemed to work out so well. Even with the symbols, there seemed to be a fairly high proportion of voters who could not understand how to mark a ballot. "Here, you do it for me," a rotund woman with a long fat braid and an infant pleaded with a well-dressed official, handing her the pen. From where I stood, I couldn't tell whether the official marked the woman's preferred candidate or not. Neither could the woman herself, and that was precisely the problem.

Jeannie walked past and joined me. "Doesn't look so secret, does it?" I mused, tapping one of the "Your Vote is Secret" signs plastered on the wall behind us.

"Not so much. I ran into one of my adult ed students and she said that an election official had asked her whom she had voted for immediately afterwards."

"Still, you have to admit they are trying. Putting symbols on the ballot was at least an attempt. And I haven't seen anyone turned away."

"Baby steps," she said. "Baby steps."

By the next day, most of the votes had been counted, and Lucio was declared the winner. Jimmy Carter, who had led a delegation of election observers to Ecuador, declared that the election was reasonably free and fair. For a third-world election, it probably was.

"Are you happy with the result?" I asked the women in the laundry room, as I shivered in a skirt while waiting for my clothes to dry. I had just one pair of pants left, and I wore them six days a week; on the seventh day—laundry day—I wore my only skirt and cursed the cold mountain air.

The plump one—the mother of Wilson, one of my *nivelación* boys—shrugged and pursed her lips. She was a gregarious woman with broad cheekbones and a blunt, earthy sense of humor. "Not really. It'll just be more of the same. Corruption. Mismanagement. Ecuadorians have no idea how to govern a country."

Her colleague was a slightly younger woman with long chestnut brown hair and sad brown eyes. Timid and mousy, she kept to herself and rarely smiled. She had been folding faded T-shirts and boxer shorts with robotic precision, but now she stopped abruptly. Her stubby, work-worn fingers absentmindedly fingered the thin cotton as her big brown eyes studied me intently. She wrinkled her nose and squinted, and I could tell she was mulling something over. "Would you consider staying on as President?"

"President of Ecuador?" I was surprised, and more than surprised, confused. Why would anyone want a foreigner running her country? Such a thought would never cross an American's mind. We think Armageddon is nigh when some Koreans buy the local auto parts factory.

She nodded slowly, and her colleague smiled knowingly and nodded along.

"No," I said, searching for a polite way to turn them down. "For one thing, I'm not from here, and I'm not all that familiar with your politics, and with the issues. For another," I added, "I think it would be a serious infringement of Ecuador's sovereignty to have a foreigner as president."

They looked confused by this last statement, and the younger woman furrowed her brow. "What about one of the other volunteers? What about Sarah? I like Sarah."

"I like Sarah, too," Wilson's mom chimed in. "Of course any of them would do. I just want an American President."

I shook my head, and they looked disappointed. "None of the volunteers can run for President," I explained. "The President must be an Ecuadorian citizen. Just like in the United States, the President must be an American citizen. In fact, the American President has to be born in the United States."

Looking dejected, they silently handed me my pink pillowcase, now stuffed with small bundle of neatly folded clothes. "*Gracias*," I said as I hugged the pillowcase to my chest. I could feel my jeans through the thin material; they were still hot from the dryer, and I was eager to rush home and put them on.

"Wait!" the younger woman called as I was walking out the door. I turned around and saw a smug, satisfied smile spreading across her delicate features. Her eyes were no longer sad. "To be ruled by an American President you have to be an American citizen, right?"

"Right."

"Then the solution is very simple."

"It is?"

She smiled and crossed her arms across her chest. "All we have to do is ask the United States to annex us."

CHAPTER SIX

A few days later, I learned yet another lesson in democracy: never ask a sixth grader to vote on anything.

At first, consulting them about the destination of our next fieldtrip had seemed like a good idea. "We could go to the planetarium or the museum," I cooed in my most enthralled, learning-is-fun teacher voice, hoping that this would inspire reasoned debate about the relative merits of ogling meteors versus shrunken heads.

Cristina looked up from her manicure, and we awaited her verdict as she carefully inspected a nail. "Museums are boring," she pronounced in her most authoritative voice, as though she were giving expert testimony. Her acolytes nodded vigorously in agreement.

"No, they're not. Not this one anyway—it has lots of solid gold Inca headdresses and even a few shrunken heads, I think."

"That's just gross, Maureen," Carmen said, wrinkling her nose.

"Really, Maureen," Cristina said in her I'm-so-disappointed-in-you voice.

We sat in silence for a moment. Cristina and Carmen gave each other a meaningful look, and Cristina elbowed Carmen gently.

Carmen cleared her throat and looked very solemn. "Actually," she said, "we have already decided where we want to go."

"You have?"

"Yes," she said solemnly. "We want to go to..."

She paused dramatically and the options raced through my head. The zoo? The pool? The movies?

"McDonald's."

"McDonald's?" I couldn't believe my ears. Really?

"Yes," she said. "That is what we want to do."

Six long, dark faces nodded in agreement. It was a unanimous vote, and I knew there was no point in arguing, so I reluctantly agreed. They erupted into cheers. "You're the best teacher ever, Maureen," Cristina gushed.

"Ronald McDonald, Ronald McDonald, Ronald McDonald, Ronald McDonald," Carmen warbled in a strange, sing-songy chant, and the other girls joined in, holding hands and jumping up and down.

I made a mental note: shrunken heads are out and Ronald McDonald is in.

On Saturday at noon, I picked them up at the downtown center. They were all there, permission slips in hand, except Cristina, for whom the girls insisted that we wait. So we sat on the steps and waited, bemoaning that our pink lip gloss-clad leader, arbiter of the cool and uncool, was nowhere in sight. At last, I convinced them that Cristina was not coming. They sighed and moaned like all the great Latin American *telenovela* divas (except poor tortured Dolores) and then resolved to go on with the excursion, difficult as it would be. Secretly, I was pleased that Cristina would not be joining us.

A red and white bus belching plumes of soot swung around the corner and slowed ever so slightly. The girls ran alongside and leapt gracefully on board, and I did the same. My long jump had definitely improved. I slid into the seat behind the driver and sat by the window; I figured Dolores would take the aisle seat. But to my amazement, Carmen sat across from me and motioned for Dolores to sit next to her. Dolores stood in the aisle for a moment, staring at Carmen and rubbing the corner of her eye. I could tell she was wondering if this was some kind of trick. But Carmen seemed sincere, and so Dolores warily took her place next to Carmen. "Can I braid your hair?" Carmen asked her in a raspy half-whisper.

Dolores's eyes widened. Yesterday, she had been a pariah so reviled that the other girls wouldn't let her within ten feet of them. Today, the second most popular girl in class was willing to confer on her the ultimate mark of social acceptance for sixth grade girls everywhere. Finally, Dolores nodded, and Carmen began to divide her thick, blue-black hair into three rope-like sections. Carmen didn't comment on the large, plum-colored bruise revealed as she lifted Dolores's thick locks off the nape of the neck, and if she spied any lice eggs, she didn't remark on that either. "You have such nice, shiny hair," was all she said. Dolores and I exchanged a small conspiratorial smile.

"*Bajamos!*" I shouted to the skinny, teenaged driver's assistant, and the driver slammed on his brakes.

Across stately Parque Carolina we skipped, linked arm in spindly arm, past majestic trees with light-colored papery bark and great heaving limbs, past love struck teens canoodling in the shade. Kicking up huge billowing dust clouds as we went, we laughed so hard it hurt. Even Dolores looked radiantly happy.

As we approached a boy in a wheelchair, the girls respectfully slowed to a walk. He stared out at us, unblinking, his head uncomfortably slumped on his right shoulder. Someone had left him there without even bothering to prop his head up. Next to him was a crude, misspelled cardboard sign with the words "Paralyzed Please Help" scrawled in red crayon, and an old empty shoebox. Drool ran down his chin and dripped onto his jeans. I looked around for a relative hovering somewhere in the background, but he seemed to be completely alone, dumped on the side of the road as a pathetic, money-making spectacle.

"*Buenos días,*" I said softly, touching his hand. His pupils darted frantically. It was heartbreaking to see how much he wanted to communicate, but couldn't, imprisoned in his stiff, frail body.

Carmen dropped a nickel into his bucket. "We should bring him some of our French fries later," Lilian said solemnly, wide-eyed.

"Or maybe part of a hamburger," suggested another. I was pleasantly surprised by the sudden generosity of girls who, on a normal day, would fight to be first in line to somewhere as mundane as the patio.

We left the boy and continued across the park. The minute we stepped onto the parking lot, the girls broke into a run. "We're here! We're here!" Carmen squealed.

"I'm going to McDonald's just like my sister did last year with one of the volunteers!"

"I want a Happy Meal!"

"Me too!"

"I want to go on the slide!"

I opened the door and we were greeted with a completely unnecessary blast of air-conditioning. A seemingly endless line of patrons with expensive wristwatches and bottle-blond hair, all waiting patiently for their Big Macs, looked up in horror as a mass of screaming girls surged towards them.

"I'm first on the slide!" Carmen shouted.

"I'm after Carmen!" Lilian screamed.

"And I'm after Lilian!"

"Girls, try to be a little quieter!" I admonished them, embarrassed, but they paid no attention.

When I arrived at the play area a moment later, the girls were already shooting out of the plastic yellow covered slide, hanging upside down from the miniature jungle-gym, and crawling through a fluorescent purple tunnel. Looking nervously at the sign that said "Children must be under 8 years old" and the one next to it, which said "Please be respectful of the other patrons," I winced as Lilian shot out of the slide and emitted a bloodcurdling scream. "Girls, aren't you hungry? Shouldn't we get in line?"

"No," Carmen pouted. "I've been waiting three years to go to McDonald's. My sister Elena went two years ago with the volunteer Ricardo, and my sister Elsa went last year with the volunteer Roberto. Now it's my turn."

And thus began a litany of stories of older sisters and brothers privileged enough to have stepped foot in McDonald's. Apparently one had not really lived until one had eaten fried beef product and shot out of a vinyl tunnel at warp speed.

"And it was the best, most fun thing she ever did," Lilian was reciting breathlessly to no one in particular.

"My sister talks about it all the time. All the time!" Julia interjected.

"Okay," I relented. "Just try and keep it down."

Forty minutes, countless dirty looks, one scratch, and three cases of rug burn later, I was at last able to extricate the girls from the play area. "Would you like a hamburger, a cheeseburger, or Chicken Nuggets?" I asked as we stood at the end of the line.

"*Una hamburguesa!*" Lilian shouted jubilantly.

"Do you know what that is?"

"No."

"It's beef."

"What animal does it come from?"

"A cow."

"Oh. Maybe I want Chicken Nuggets. What's that?"

"*Pollo*," I said, feeling slightly complicit in the food industry's creative definition of what constitutes chicken, or any meat for that matter.

"Okay, I want that." I ordered six Happy Meals and a Big Mac, and we took them to a table in the far corner.

Carmen took one bite of her cheeseburger and dropped it on the table like a rock. "I don't like it," she admitted, genuinely shocked. Her beloved Ronald McDonald had let her down.

After lunch, the girls begged to ride the escalators. Riding the escalators had become part of the field trip circuit; it was akin to taking a bunch of American junior high students to an amusement park. A few weeks before, Jeannie's students had been escorted out of the mall by two humorless security guards who threatened to arrest them if they came back. Jeannie was indignant and threatened to mount a boycott of the mall, but the guards were nonplussed. "It's not like anyone you know has money to spend anyway," they taunted her as she stomped off to the bus stop. She gave them the finger.

I had my own reasons for enthusiastically embracing Jeannie's "boycott". For one thing, entering the mall was a discombobulating experience: it was as though a glitzy shopping center in Los Angeles had been swept up in a cyclone and plunked down in the middle of an Ecuadorian parking lot. There was an assortment of expensive jewelry and clothing stores, a multiplex featuring a bewildering array of violent American movies dubbed into Spanish, and what was quite possibly the only skating rink in the world within fifteen miles of the equator. It was a cruelly ironic monument to consumerism, and I always felt a bit guilty as I slunk out the door, plastic bag in hand.

The other reason was that the mall had also been the scene of many humiliations of my own. It was there that I had stood in line for the multiplex with one of my fourteen year-old boys, mysteriously wearing my oh-so-glamorous tortoise-rimmed Ecuadorian sunglasses and nervously thrusting my hair in my face.

Under my breath, I was praying that none of the Ecuadorian teachers had had the bright idea to bring their kids to the movies today. "Two tickets to 'Harry Potter,'" I had whispered to the bemused woman at the ticket counter, feeling like a pedophile. "He's my student," I had babbled on. "Really. I invited a whole bunch of kids, but he's the only one who showed up. I guess the others didn't have enough for bus fare." She hadn't seemed particularly convinced.

It was also the setting of an ill-fated shopping expedition prompted by an episode in which I had reached up to put a math problem on the board and suddenly found my bra pooled around my waist; my extreme weight loss had had a rather deflating effect. "Do you have anything, um, smaller?" I had asked after trying on at least twenty without success.

The saleswoman had glanced at my chest and then looked up at me, incredulous. "Do you even need one?"

"I work with teenage boys."

Her lips had formed a perfect circle, and a tomato red nail had tapped the register. "Well try a training bra then," she had said. "But I am not sure if that is even going to work."

And last but not least, it was where a rather comic quest for a new pair of jeans had ended. "*Guácala! Guácala!*" the well-meaning salesgirl had shouted in horror as I emerged from the dressing room. The other customers had gathered around and echoed her assessment. "*Guácala,*" they had murmured. The Quichua word for "ugly," "guácala" was one of the few indigenous words consistently used by both white and indigenous Ecuadorians; the others were "*chuchaqui*" (hung over) and "*guagua*" (baby). The amateur linguist in me found it sad and more than a little horrifying that Ecuadorian slang seemed to reflect the common view that indigenous people were ugly, drunk, baby-making machines, but Ecuadorians didn't seem to think anything of it.

"But I like them," I had protested. "They don't cling like every other pair I have tried on."

"Try the Size Small back on," the salesgirl had pleaded with me. "You looked so cute in them. More like Christina Aguilera, and less like a grandma."

But I had insisted and after an hour of arguing with her and the other customers, I had finally emerged with my grandma jeans, victorious.

And so now it was with heavy heart that I broke Jeannie's boycott and led my charges into the mall's posh department store. They stood in wonderment at the base of the *"gradas eléctricas"* (electric stairs) and watched well-heeled patrons blithely step on and off the faintly squeaking magic stairs.

Lilian pointed at the grooves in the step. "It looks like teeth," she whispered.

"It's actually very easy to ride," Carmen said proudly. "Here, let me show you." She tossed her hair behind her back and lightly brushed her palm against the railing with studied casualness. I almost expected her to extend her pinky, as if she were having tea with the queen. "I came here last year with Marco," she explained, pausing for effect as a few of the other girls bristled with envy. "Now the trick you see is to lift your leg a little bit higher than you normally would." She lifted one leg and glided onto the step. "See? It's very simple after you practice for a bit." Beaming down at us, she ascended amidst home furnishings and accessories.

Trembling from excitement and fear, the other girls stood in a clump, clutching each other. "Are you ready?" I gently coaxed Lilian.

She nodded, but looked terrified. "I can do this, I can do this, I can do this," she whispered over and over, like a mantra. She placed a hand on the handrail and recoiled as she felt it slipping away. She bit her lip.

"It's okay," I said. "Just do it fast. Don't think about it too much."

She placed her hand on the handrail again, watched it slip away, lifted her hand, and placed it gently on the handrail once more. With one final terrified backwards glance, she took a deep breath, lifted her leg, and lurched forward. For a moment, she wobbled. But then she grabbed hold of the handrail and straightened herself, a shy, self-satisfied smile spreading across her face. Her amazed classmates applauded loudly.

Now that Lilian had proven that even a newbie could master the art of riding an escalator, all of the girls clamored for their turn. And so they rode the escalators up and up and down, twenty times or more, cheering loudly each time they successfully landed on the first step.

Flush from our grand adventure, we wandered through the mall aimlessly, marveling at the incredible variety of more or less useless consumer goods being offered at what to these girls seemed like exorbitant prices. After an hour or so, Julia asked if we could go. "Seeing all of these things makes me want to buy them," she said, "which makes me want to ask my mom to buy them, but I know she can't and asking her will just make her sad."

"Julia is right, girls," I said gently. "We've seen enough expensive, ridiculous things for the day."

Carmen bit her lip. "Let's go see if that boy is still there."

We retraced our steps, but he was gone. The girls looked a little dejected; they were all set to do another good deed, and there was none to be done.

We went to the park and assembled our Happy Meal toys. "This is the most fabulous toy I have ever had," Lilian gushed. "I'm going to share it with my brother."

Julia lay on her back and looked up at the sky dreamily. "Guess what, Maureen?"

"What?"

"I'm going to go to college!"

"Really?" It was the first time all year I had heard any of my students put college forth as goal. The vast majority of them did not even plan on going to high school.

"Yep. Just like my brother. He's studying at the university now."

I stared at Julia. Could this be true? I was not aware of any Center graduates going to college. It seemed unthinkable. Not only did our families lack the means, but I knew that the Madres and the Padre actively discouraged college. In their view, a college education was an expensive dead end, not to mention a selfish indulgence. Your family needs all the income it can get, they would say. Going to college is just a way to weasel out of family obligations. And they didn't consider it an investment in the future. Ecuador didn't have enough demand to employ all of the college graduates it produced, and in any case the quality of its education was generally abysmal.

In a sense, of course, they were right. The educational quality of these institutions was suspect, I discovered shortly after my arrival. So many of our teachers had trouble figuring out where to put the periods in a paragraph that the Madres had organized a Saturday session on punctuation. It was less than successful.

It was also true that a college education did not necessarily guarantee a good income. Our teachers were paid only two hundred dollars a month—almost twice the official minimum wage, but still less than what was needed for a middle class standard of living. And that was when they weren't paid with an I.O.U. Once they didn't get paid for seven months while the Madres waited anxiously for the donations to pour in.

And yet some part of me really wanted to believe that Julia was telling me the truth. Even if it was irrational, impractical, even selfish, I wanted a family to defy this defeatist logic. I wanted them to believe in the future, believe that not every day had to be the same boring grind of survival. I wanted to know that someone wanted to learn for the sake of learning, for the pure joy of it. Have them learn a trade, the Madres and the Padre repeated like a mantra. Read instruction manuals with them instead of literature, Don Rodrigo would plead with me. But something inside of me always screamed no, don't listen to them, kids. The future will never come if you always prepare to live the status quo.

And Julia made me believe. There was not a trace of a giggle on her lips; there was no mischievous look in her eye. She looked earnest and sincere, impressed by the seriousness of her goal but also excited. Exactly the way she should look. I believe, Julia, I believe, I said with my eyes, but out loud all I said was, "I hope you do."

The sun began to slip beneath the horizon, infusing the earth with its warm red glow. Back across the park we skipped, a little bit more worldly and quite a bit more charitable than we had been the day before. "I can't believe I rode an escalator today," Dolores exclaimed, squeezing my hand tightly. "Did you have a nice time, Maureen?"

I glanced at Dolores and her braid. I watched college-bound Julia bound joyfully through the grass, and Carmen, my budding philanthropist, clutch her carefully wrapped leftovers to her chest. I didn't know if it was the absence of Cristina, or the fact that they for once felt worthy of descending from their miserable hovels in the hillside slums and enjoying themselves like any other pre-teen girl, but something about today had transformed them. It was as if all of their hurt, their shame, their self-hatred, and their envy had been stripped away. And without all of that, they were no longer petty or brutal, snobbish or vain. They were just little girls.

It wouldn't last, I knew. Tomorrow the same old fights, the same old rivalries would resurface. Today would have to be enough.

"I had a great time, Dolores," I finally murmured. "I will remember this day forever."

CHAPTER SEVEN

The Fiestas of Quito are held the week of December 5th to commemorate the founding of Quito. Of course, December 5th is really the anniversary of the Spanish re-founding of Quito because, as the graffiti next to the bullring attests, "The Spanish didn't found Quito"; Quito was already the capital of the Quitus. This historical fact, however, is of little importance to the city's tourism industry, which has turned the event into a weeklong extravaganza of bullfights and chiva-ing.

Chiva-ing consists of renting an open-air, double-decker party bus (*chiva*), jumping up and down for hours in an alcohol-induced frenzy—while hoping your driver is in a better state—and pulling over at random moments to square dance. Eager to partake of this "cultural" experience, the other volunteers and I, plus assorted Center staff members (but *not* the Madres and Padre) and Ecuadorian friends, rolled our way through Quito's nearly deserted streets like an army of Mexican jumping beans, while the *chiva's* "band"—an off-key trumpet player and a drummer thumping his enormous drum like the Energizer bunny—played the same song about Quito over and over again for two and a half hours. The Center's doctor led the revelers in a lusty cheer about drinking until we were all up to our balls in liquor, or something like that, while we drank, blew our plastic whistles, and waved mini-Ecuadorian flags.

The party season really began, though, with the lavish *quinceañera* of one of my ninth-grade students. Silvia Villa, one of the prettiest and most popular girls in the class, was turning fifteen and her parents intended to celebrate this rite of passage—historically the advent of womanhood, when girls were first considered available for marriage—in style. The whole junior high buzzed with excitement.

"*Profesora*, are you going to Silvia's *quinceañera*?" one of the girls shrieked with excitement as she greeted me before class.

"Of course. Are you?"

"If my mom lets me."

"Are you going to have a *quinceañera* later this year?"

She shook her head.

"Why not?"

"No money. Besides, the Madre and Padre are against it. They say it's a waste of money and silly, anyway."

Yeah, I thought, but they would be against dancing too if it weren't for the fact that the Methodists thought of it first. Wisely, however, I bit my tongue.

"Ooooooh, I am going to wear my new pink dress and heels and wear my hair up!" another squealed. "Teacher, what are you going to wear?"

Ten eager young faces, flushed with excitement, turned to survey me. "Wear something that shows your midriff, Maureen," one of my girls instructed me patiently, as if talking to a small child. She wrinkled her nose. "You always look so...*dowdy*."

"Yes, something that shows your midriff!" interjected another, animatedly. "And something low cut. You know..." She thrust her prepubescent chest out.

"Well, I don't know..."

"You have to be sexy, Maureen!"

"Absolutely!"

"Wear heels!"

"Wear something red!"

"Don't wear something with holes in it." I looked down at my shirt and noticed the fraying hem and the little hole starting near my top button. It was another laundry casualty.

"Don't look like a teacher!" offered another, sounding disgusted. "It makes you look so...*old*."

Mercifully, it was time for class to begin, so I could stop pondering the wisdom of their fashion advice and start lecturing them about prepositions. The class, however, was even less interested than usual in the lesson. The girls were doodling sketches of women in evening gowns and showing them to each other. Silvia was daydreaming, while her friends gazed admiringly at her. The girls were checking the boys out, sizing up which ones might ask them to dance, and the boys were checking the girls out, making a mental list of the girls they would like to dance with and those they would actually have enough courage to ask to dance. I tried incorporating the vibe into the lesson—"Carlos wants to dance *with* Lupe, but Lupe is dancing *with* Pedro," "Juan sends a love letter *to* Silvia," etc., but it was only partially successful. My teaching skills were no match for teenage hormones.

The day of *quinceañera* did not begin auspiciously. The other invited volunteers and I spent two hours on rickety city buses, missed our bus stop, and ended up running helter-skelter up the mountainside of a shantytown in search of an elusive church while pursued by mangy dogs. Every time we paused to ask directions, the residents would just keep shouting "*Arriba! Arriba!*" and gesturing towards the top of the mountain. It wasn't very helpful. Then the heavens opened up and it began to pour.

At last we stumbled across a church, an ugly, concrete monstrosity perched on a ridge, the type of church hailed as a masterpiece of modern architecture for the first year of its existence and then promptly ridiculed as a monument to bad taste. We burst in, wet and bedraggled, and found ourselves in what appeared to be the middle of a wedding. But on second glance, the bride *did* look familiar....

Silvia stood at the altar, enveloped in yards of poufy pink taffeta and flanked by her coterie of friends. Their expressions ranged from awe to envy. Maricela chewed her lip nervously and tapped her foot; Katrina preened and cast a backwards glance at Miguel each time she tossed her hair. They all wore brand-new matching bridesmaid dresses. Judging by the way they kept smoothing the shiny fabric over their hips and surreptitiously admiring their shoes, I could tell that they were mightily impressed by their appearance.

"They look so grown-up," I whispered to Jeannie.

"Looks are deceiving."

The priest droned on with his uninspired sermon, covering the time-worn themes of responsibility, respect, and faith, and Silvia seemed to take it all very seriously, nodding at the appropriate times. Then they brought out a big, pink, cushy chair. No ordinary chair, it was elevated off the ground, flanked by big heavy armrests, and decorated with all kinds of pink baubles. It looked like a throne that had been snatched from a high school *Cinderella* production.

Silvia sat dutifully in the chair while her parents approached the altar, knelt before her, and removed her shoes. They whisked out a pair of bubble gum pink, six-inch heels and slid them on her feet. This ritual, we were informed, signified the advent of womanhood.

How appropriate and yet disturbing, I thought, as Silvia teetered down the steps back to her pew, beaming. Ecuadorian womanhood was more often than not solely about attracting and pleasing men and having children—essentially sex and the result of having sex. One's status as a woman was not enhanced by having a job, or being financially independent, or owning a home or a bank account, or making one's own decisions, or being a source of wisdom and strength for one's friends and family. If a woman arrived at the age of twenty-five or twenty-six without being married, she was considered an old maid for life, and basically a failure as a woman. It was enough to strike fear in the heart of any Ecuadorian teenage girl.

The Mass concluded and we marched out of the church. Silvia's family had rented a school bus to take us to back their home, and I slid into a seat next to a plump woman with wiry curls and broad cheekbones. Leaning against the window, she traced the raindrops as they zigzagged across the pane. Turning towards me, she smiled shyly. "Isn't this a wonderful celebration?"

"Fabulous," I said. "Silvia looked just beautiful on the altar."

"I wish I could have given my daughters such a beautiful celebration. But you know how it is....*No hay plata*." She rubbed her thumb and forefinger together in a gesture I had seen a million times: brown-skinned flesh on brown-skinned flesh, with nary a fleck of silver (*plata*) in between. It was a phrase that I had at first found jarring, a terribly antiquated figure of speech that smacked of medieval mercantilism, of Pizarro and Cortez. But the longer I spent in Ecuador, the more sense it made, and I had come to accept it for the shorthand it was—a quasi-punctuation mark in a culture of want.

The motor groaned beneath us. The wheels spun in place, spewing a thick sludge of chocolate-colored mud onto the church plaza and sending the soggy passengers bumping into one another.

Silvia's girlfriends screamed, and the boys laughed. "This is awesome!" a masculine voice shouted from the back of the bus.

The driver shut off the engine, waited a moment, and tried again. This time, the engine sputtered for a moment, then settled into sonorous rumble as the wheels at last gained traction. We rocked forward, then back, then surged forward once more. As the rusting carcass heaved forward once more, scraping the baseboards, the bus wobbled, then pitched sharply to the right. Laughter erupted as the Ecuadorians slammed into their neighbors.

One of the older women stood up and clapped her hands authoritatively. "Okay, everyone to the left!"

Everyone moved as far to the left as possible, and the bus listed leftwards. She frowned. "Okay, we overdid it a little. Ten people move back to the right."

After a few more careful calibrations, we at last achieved equilibrium. The bus took off down the street to thunderous applause, careened over and around the shantytown's rain-soaked hills, and came to a stop in front of a modest concrete home with a covered front patio. "It's very nice," my seatmate said admiringly. "Big, too."

A quick house tour led by Silvia confirmed what my companion has said: in comparison to most of our members' homes, it *was* big. Attached to the patio were a kitchen and a tiny bathroom with, to my pleasant surprise, a real functioning toilet. Inside were a living room with a single lime green couch and a tiny TV and a bedroom crammed with mattresses. The floor was a gray concrete slab and the walls were cinderblock.

Silvia finished her tour, and Jeannie and I went out on the patio. Huddled together for warmth, we sat on rusted-out folding chairs against the wall, staring out at the flooded street. The storm had worn a channel in the dirt road, and now a torrent of cloudy water rushed down the hillside, dragging diapers and Fanta cans with it, gathering speed as it rushed down to the valley below.

Jeannie sipped watermelon-flavored Fanta from a paper cup. They had all kinds of strange soft drinks in Ecuador: strawberry-flavored, passion fruit-flavored, even best-selling Inca Cola, which tasted like bubble gum to me but was reputedly the elixir of the gods. Some communities in Peru reportedly used it as a libation to Mother Earth during sacred indigenous ceremonies. Usually, Jeannie would give a detailed assessment of each new flavor she tried: its taste, its smell, its fizziness factor. It was almost like wine tasting for her. But today she was strangely silent and morose.

"Are you okay?" I asked.

She shifted uncomfortably in her seat. "Remember little Juanito, from my first-grade health class?" I didn't, but I nodded anyway. She didn't seem in the mood for lengthy explanations. "He died last week," she said in a low, even voice. "Apparently his mother left him unattended while she went to go vote and he drowned in a cistern. It wasn't fenced in or anything." She stared straight ahead, refusing to look at me. A thin film of unshed tears clouded her eyes; if she blinked or moved ever so slightly, they would slide down her face.

I put my hand on her shoulder and squeezed gently. "I'm really sorry," was all I said. There was nothing more to say and, even if it there were, I knew Jeannie wouldn't want me to say it. She didn't want to talk about her feelings, and she didn't want to cry in public. More than anything, she didn't want me to say it was okay, because it wasn't. That would offend her sense of moral outrage, her deep sense of justice. And that was what I loved most about Jeannie: the way her toughness mingled with her deep compassion, bringing out the best of both sides. I loved her determination. She was a quiet revolutionary; she was my co-conspirator and my closest friend.

We sat in silence for a while and watched the rain. A shout or burst of laughter from inside occasionally swept through the patio and then dissipated into the damp night, swallowed by the roar of the storm. I shivered in my wet socks and wet shoes and tried to wring the muddy water from my pants leg. The bottom six inches had turned brown, and I was none too pleased. I had borrowed them.

Silvia came out onto the patio, beaming. She wore a thick gray sweatshirt over her pink party dress, and she handed us steaming bowls of chicken soup and a plate piled high with shredded chicken and *llapingachos*, potato-and-cheese pancakes. Delightfully crispy on the outside and gooey on the inside, they were my favorite Ecuadorian food. Her father watched from the doorway for a moment, smiling a quiet little smile, and then retreated back inside with Silvia.

"They seem like a very loving family," I said.

Jeannie shrugged. "From what I hear, he's an alcoholic. But he's a good drunk, I guess. A happy drunk. He doesn't beat his kids much, or at least not unless they do something really bad."

"Well that," I said as I bit into a crispy *llapingacho*, "counts for something."

A half an hour later, Jeannie and I no longer had the patio to ourselves. It was crammed with party guests, all grinning from ear to ear and plowing their way through steaming paper plates. It was the best meal most of them had had in years.

Miguel, one of my mechanics, stuck his finger in my soup and tapped the hunk of bone moored to the bottom. "Aren't you going to eat that?"

I shook my head. He reached in, pulled it out, and held it to his lips. First, he sucked off all of the juices. Then, he placed the tip between his incisors, bit off a small piece, and began to grind away. I looked around and saw that everyone else was doing the same.

"You Americans are so weird," he said. "The bone is the best part."

When every last drop of soup had been slurped and every last bone chewed, the Ecuadorians made their way to the dance floor. The teenagers only knew one step, for the most part—the shy, shuffle-to-one-side, shuffle-to-the-other step, complete with a studious avoidance of eye contact with their partner. I didn't have a partner to shuffle with, so I alternated between jumping up and down and flailing my arms and adopting a more dignified toe tap. My students thought it was hilarious.

From time to time, I shot a surreptitious glance at Silvia, who was dancing shyly with a few of the male volunteers and occasionally a relative. To me, she didn't look any more like a woman than she had the day before.

It wasn't long before the disc jockey, Roberto, pulled the plug on the Spanish teen pop and tapped the mike. "*Ahoooooooooooooooooora,*" he intoned in his best radio announcer voice, slicking back his shiny, blue-black hair like a matinee idol, "it is time to remove the garter." He was in his early thirties and, despite being married to a fellow member of the Center and having two small children, had a reputation as something of a ladies' man.

A ripple of excitement went through the crowd. Roberto nodded and winked at one of the "bridesmaids." *"Que viva la quinceañera!"* he shouted.

"Que viva!" the crowd roared and raised its plastic cups in a toast.

Ringed by a circle of revelers, Silvia waited while gleefully nervous adolescent boys slid the garter up the legs of her seemingly endless supply of "bridesmaids" and then down. Up and down. Pass to the next awkward boy and nervous girl. Up and down. It was a blur of ruffled skirts, quivering hands, shy smiles and giggles.

Finally, the garter made its way back to Silvia. As Silvia's boyfriend rolled the garter off the last bridesmaid's leg and onto Silvia's ankle, Roberto stopped him. "No, no, no. *Con los dientes,"* he crooned seductively.

I looked over at this gangly, pimply boy, horrified. Was Roberto really egging him on to drag the garter up Silvia's leg with his teeth?

I looked over at Paul, who had his head in his hands. He slowly shook his head back and forth. "I can't believe this guy," he hissed in my ear. Pushing his way through the crowd, he protested loudly to anyone who would listen this was a highly inappropriate ritual for a bunch of fourteen and fifteen-year-olds. "They're just children!" he shouted.

But the Ecuadorians swatted him off, like a harmless fly, with a bemused look and a shrug. They saw nothing strange in this ritual. Even Silvia's parents wore expressions that were pleasantly blank and passive.

When the boyfriend began pulling the garter up past Silvia's knee, his head buried beneath her skirt, Roberto at last intervened. He concluded the ritual with another lusty cry of *"Viva la quinceañera!,"* and Silvia's parents joined in, wearing the same blank, beatific expressions as before.

Then they brought out the hard liquor. It was stored in two huge plastic vats, and it was the kind of alcohol that everyone warned could make you go blind. "It's just like rubbing alcohol from the medicine cabinet," Paul announced after taking a sip. "Plus it has an added medicinal benefit: it clears your sinuses right up."

Carmen's parents made the rounds, beaming as they poured it liberally into each of Carmen's friend's cups. It dribbled down the sides, and soon the concrete floor became sticky. Then came the Jell-O shots, and then more rounds of homemade liquor. The dancing degenerated into random stomping, and collisions on the dance floor became increasingly frequent. Most of the fourteen and fifteen-year-olds retreated to the sidelines in a stupor, and Roberto looked a little glassy-eyed too.

I retreated as well, taking a seat next to Paul, who was by now exceedingly drunk. "The cook's daughter didn't even make it to fifteen," he shouted into my eardrum. His eyes were puffy and bloodshot, and his breath smelled of cheap whiskey.

I had never seen him so angry, and it frightened me. Could this be the very same Paul who teased me about Darwin and spent his weekends dancing at No-Bar? I wasn't exactly sure what to say, so I settled on nodding sympathetically and murmuring, "I know."

"Pregnant at fourteen, married at fourteen," he railed, jabbing his finger in the air violently. "Kicked out of the Center. Three kids by nineteen. Abusive husband. What kind of a life of that?" He stared at me accusingly, as if I could somehow have prevented that, and then lurched forwards unsteadily. I gently propped him up, and he straightened himself with exaggerated dignity. "We're friends, right?"

"Right."

"So I can tell you a secret, right?"

"Sure."

"And you'll keep it, right?

"Right."

"A couple of weeks ago one of my favorite ninth grade girls came to me. She's a real cute girl, very sweet, a pretty good student in my English class. Always making jokes. Always laughing. Anyways, she comes up to me before class and she asks if she can speak to me alone, so I say 'sure,' thinking it's about a grade or maybe she needs a little help studying for the upcoming test. But no. She asks for money. Lots of money. Three hundred dollars. I ask her what it's for, but she won't tell me. I ask her if someone in her family is sick, and she says no. I can't get anything out of her. Finally, I tell her that if she can't tell me what's it's for, I can't help her."

"And?"

"Three weeks later she is kicked out of the Center for being pregnant."

"Oh."

"Yeah." He tilted his head all the way back, and took a long, slow sip, closing his eyes.

The wind picked up, and the sound of rushing water grew louder. The rain began to fall in great shimmering sheets, and deep thunderous rumbles rolled across the landscape, each louder than the one before, building to a dramatic crescendo that echoed off the mountains. A strong gust lifted a corner of the canvas roof and sent it billowing skyward for a moment before abruptly letting go. The guests laughed, and a shrill voice rang out over storm. *"Que viva la quinceañera!"*

The revelers dutifully raised their cups. *"Que viva la quinceañera,"* they mumbled into their cups.

I looked over at Paul. He did not join in the cry, and he did not raise his cup in a toast. He just stared straight ahead. Slowly, deliberately, he crushed his cup in his fist and hurled it out onto the street. He shook his head and in a voice that only I could hear said exactly what was on my mind: "I don't know why they are in such a hurry to grow up."

CHAPTER EIGHT

It was Christmas at last. As we rumbled along the road to Huangopolo, Madre Josefina's shrill soprano pierced through the more sonorous alto and bass voices.

Silent night, Holy night
All is calm, All is bright
Round yon virgin, Mother and Child...

It was the first time all year I had sung in English, and for some reason I found it immensely comforting. For once, there were no obligatory hand gestures, Holy Spirits hitting us in the form of lightning bolts, or dumbed-down lyrics for the barely literate. There were no children turning around in the middle of Mass and telling me I "sang weird" because I didn't have the same breathy, reedy voice that every Ecuadorian seemed to have. It was truly peaceful and calm.

Outside the stars shone brightly over the dark landscape. Houses became fewer and far between as we wound our way down steep embankments and over hills. Behind us lay the city, silent and dark in its poverty; far ahead of us to the east, the jungle.

We came to a stop alongside Huangopolo's quaint town square and its hulking colonial-era church. Padre served as Huangopolo's parish priest in addition to his duties at the Center. Madre called it his "Indian parish," which seemed like a rather misleading appellation to me; after all, the parishioners were no more indigenous than the majority of the people we served at the Center. But Madre insisted it was an "Indian parish" and that was that. Since Padre almost never spoke, it was hard to know what he called it.

In the cobblestone courtyard, throngs of dark-skinned peasants milled about. Teenagers shyly flirted with one another, while men in tattered woolen sweaters proudly showed off their babies to relatives and friends. They fussily arranged their child's clothes, and their friends smiled admiringly.

On closer inspection, I saw that most of these babies were not flesh and blood at all, but limp, lifeless dolls. Some were one-eyed and others had limbs hanging on by just a thread. The plastic *muñecas* were definitely supposed to be Caucasian, with startlingly blue eyes, tiny button noses, and strange orangey complexions. Those with cotton bodies were of more ambiguous origin: stained with the sweat and grime, smeared with grease, it was hard to discern their original color. And then there were the freakish hybrids—stiff-bodied, tangerine-colored figurines with a random cinnamon-hued cotton appendage; well-loved soft-bodied dolls with one pupil glassy and cerulean and the other black and almond-shaped.

As I was inspecting a particularly interesting repair job—a fat Cabbage Patch Kid with two green buttons for eyes and a royal blue cape—a short, round man with silvery stubble and whiskers suddenly embraced me. His grip was strong, and he mumbled something unintelligible in my ear, smiling rapturously. The stench of human sweat was overpowering.

Madre caught my eye and strode purposefully across the courtyard, over and around the parishioners squatting on the cracked white stones. She tugged at his sleeve. *"Déjala en paz, Ramón,"* she said in a low, soothing voice, and he released me.

She motioned for me to follow her. "Don't worry about him," she said, waving her arm dismissively. "He's just the village idiot."

We passed through the impressive stone doorway and into the barren interior of the church. The mood inside was more like that of a refugee camp than a solemn celebration. Families squatted on the floor, and I was nearly overpowered by the stench of human sweat, urine, and animals. Dogs with matted coats brushed past my legs, and the din was deafening.

Madre Josefina instructed me to stand near the front of altar with the other volunteers. "That's the only way you'll hear anything," she warned.

We stood dutifully to the side as Padre walked slowly down the aisle with his dignified, slightly stooping gait. The choir belted out an Ecuadorian *villancico*, but even they could not drown out the racket.

"I guess paying attention is optional," Jeannie shouted in my ear.

"Evidently."

Padre cleared his throat loudly and began leading the congregation in the Act of Contrition. *"Confieso ante Dios todopoderoso y ante Ustedes, hermanos y hermanas, que he pecado…"*

"Ay, Juan, qué gusto!" a barrel-chested man in the front row bellowed, thumping a middle-aged man on the back.

"Igualmente! Qué tal tu hijita?" his friend chattered on.

I put a hand over my left ear and tried to drown out the fragmented conversations, the hearty handshakes, the occasional trill of laughter, the barking dogs, and the screaming babies.

"POR MI CULPA, POR MI CULPA, POR MI GRAN CULPA," Padre roared. During Spanish Mass, for some reason, each "culpa" was accompanied by a loud thump to the chest, as if mass self-inflicted violence would somehow expiate the guilt. Today, though, Padre really beat his chest—more in anger, it seemed, than guilt.

Agitated, Padre sped up, leaving half of the congregation to continue their socializing and the other half several sentences behind him. When he finished, he pounded his fist on the pulpit. "Everyone shut up long enough to hear the Word of God!" he exhorted the congregation.

There was a moment of gratifying silence. But then the conversations began to bubble up again, and Mass became one long confusing litany interspersed with Padre's exhortations to *callarse*.

When Mass ended, Padre hoarsely invited the parishioners to place their "baby Jesuses" on one of the long wooden tables that lined the walls. Padre carefully dipped his staff in a large vat, and with a quick snap of the wrist sent torrents of holy water streaming towards a grotesque tangle of limbs. Then everyone retrieved their doll, drank copious quantities of hot chocolate, and processed back to their homes, one-eyed baby Jesuses in tow.

Swinging around a hairpin turn, we squeezed through the narrow mountain pass. On our right rose a massive wall of bedrock; on our left was an almost vertical drop to the rushing stream far below. An occasional bare patch marred the velvety green slope, marking where the earth had slid away in a single shearing motion and tumbled down the precipice. Tree branches slammed through the open windows, their long, stiff leaves stinging our faces. I reached out to bend the branches back, and a rock outcropping scraped my hand. Nature in this part of the world is aggressive.

We rounded another turn, and another, and another. It was a nauseating, vertiginous descent—a blur of gray stone, twisted black asphalt, and profuse dark green vegetation, all flying past the window at odd angles. Up was down; down was up. "I think I am going to be sick," I moaned softly to Stacey, who patted my arm and began rooting through our backpacks for empty plastic bags. Stacey was one volunteer you could always count on to take care of you; she was sweet and unfailingly cheerful, almost maternal.

"Just think what a marvelous Christmas break we are going to have," she said. "Try not to think about your stomach."

I closed my eyes and tried to will away the nausea. My head throbbed with the driving salsa beat, and my heart pounded each time the driver frantically pumped the brakes. The bus sounded like a wheezing asthmatic.

Gradually the turns became gentler, and the nausea receded. Each minute, the air became heavier and warmer than the last, and a languid stillness seemed to come over the passengers. Birdcalls became louder and more frequent.

Stacey nudged me gently. "It's okay to look now," she said.

A magical landscape spread before us—thick tangles of vines, delicate orchids, bright butterflies and squawking birds. The reds were redder than red, the greens greener than green. A faint mist hovered in the air.

As we continued our gradual descent, the air became even warmer and the land flatter. The turbulent white waters slowed to a swift, but smooth, muddy brown, and finally to a sinuous black ribbon that snaked languidly through villages and farm fields. Then the banana plantations appeared, vast tracts of land stretching as far as the eye could see, dotted with great green bunches thrusting skyward. Sometimes they were covered with black plastic trash bags, marking that harvest was near.

The land was not the only thing that changed. Each village was noisier and more colorful than the last, the people brasher and less inhibited, the style of dress more and more provocative. The noses became flatter, the eyes rounder, the complexions generally lighter but also more varied. Some villagers were white, some were black, and most were somewhere in between.

In Esmeraldas, we changed buses. It was a ramshackle, rough-and-tumble town of wooden shacks with narrow porches, and it was the capital of Ecuador's northernmost coastal province, also named Esmeraldas. With its long and violent border with Colombia, it had become notorious as a center for drug trafficking. We had been warned repeatedly not to linger there.

At last we arrived in Puerto López. It too was a rather ramshackle beach town, but there was something picturesque about its sand-colored buildings in the late afternoon light. Lined with flowers and filled with more bicycles than cars, its narrow dirt lanes dead-ended at the town's beach, which was pleasant but unremarkable. Its seemingly endless expanse of sand was gray and grainy; it seemed that more animals used the beach than people. Seagulls soared high above the crashing waves, then swooped low for a bite to eat; fat hogs occasionally pranced at the water's edge as their owners trailed behind. But the sunsets were anything but ordinary: streaks of gold across the blue sky; the great golden orb growing and then sinking slowly beneath the pounding surf; shimmering swathes of crimson and lavender; and finally an endless star-studded expanse of indigo. It made Quito seem far, far away.

Stacey and I loved Puerto López. We took bicycle taxis, ate Italian food, bested rich, fat Ecuadorian tourists impractically clad in bathing suits and flip-flops on a three-hour hike to see the blue boobies (birds with big, blue webbed feet), went snorkeling, and hiked through a cloud forest in the nearby national park.

Puerto López's only negative, as far as we could tell, was its plague of *grillos* (crickets), revolting four-inch winged creatures the color of mud that had a penchant for lunging at you the moment your back was turned. It was like something out of the Bible, with literally thousands of *grillos* congregating around each streetlight. A simple stroll easily became fodder for nightmares: thoraxes crunched beneath our feet and a snaking brown line fled our advance.

The locals, however, were completely unfazed by the invasion, as I discovered while discussing hiking options with Pedro, a local guide who patiently outlined different hikes as seventeen *grillos* marched up and down his body. "You see," he said, as a *grillo* scampered across his lapel and tickled his neck with his antennae, "you can either take this route,"—he turned to indicate a path on the wall map, sweeping away a mass of entangled brown bodies with a flick of the wrist and not so much as a grimace—"or this one, which has less spectacular views but is technically easier." A *grillo* lunged from his desk and landed squarely on Pedro's nose. Pedro just wrinkled his nose, brushed off his pesky friend, and continued extolling the virtues of the national park.

Stacey and I took refuge in the hotel's swimming pool; *grillos* can't swim. What we had not considered is that another kind of local pest—the overly persistent Ecuadorian man—can.

"And where are you two lovely ladies from?" a middle-aged gentleman with salt-and-pepper hair crooned as Stacey and I stood chest-deep in the center of pool, anxiously watching the *grillos* mass on the deck. His stomach spilled out over his teensy-weensy black Speedos.

"*Los Estados Unidos*," I replied warily.

"Aha," he said, as if this were a very significant and revealing tidbit of information. I doubted that it was, however, since Stacey and I had been speaking in English for over half an hour.

"But we live in Quito now."

"Aha." There was an uncomfortable silence for a moment. "I'm Santiago," he finally said, extending his hand. "And this is my wife Linda"—he jerked a thumb towards a plump, fifty-something woman perched on the deck behind him, her feet dangling in the water—"and my younger brother Enrique." Enrique stood apart from them, leaning lazily against the side of the pool. With his smooth olive complexion, piercing dark eyes, and broad, muscular chest, it was hard to believe that he and Santiago were related.

"*Encantada*," I said, shaking their hands, and Stacey did the same. I noticed that Enrique held our hands longer than absolutely necessary.

"What are American men like?" Santiago asked, as if this were the most natural question in the world.

"*No sé*," I stammered. It was a little hard to generalize about one hundred million of them. "Tall, I guess. Well some of them are anyway. Compared to Ecuadorians, that is…"

"Tall, yes," Santiago said breezily. He seemed bored with my faltering attempt to categorize American men. "But do you like Ecuadorian men?" he pressed.

"Sometimes," I demurred. The truth was that I had a lot more experience with Ecuadorian boys than Ecuadorian men.

"Would you marry an Ecuadorian man?"

Stacey laughed nervously. "That's a funny question," she said.

"Well, would you?" Santiago's tone was still friendly and his smile still wide, but the lines around his eyes betrayed the slightest bit of impatience. Clearly he was after something. I just wasn't sure what it was.

"Probably not," I said slowly, choosing my words carefully, "but I wouldn't rule it out."

"Why do you say 'probably not'?" Enrique asked, smiling at me. He looked amused.

"Well…"

"Well what?"

"It seems that a lot of them are not faithful to their wives." I knew of at least one affair among the teachers, and from what I had heard extramarital affairs were quite commonplace. To be fair, of course, it did seem to be something on an equal opportunity sport: the mother of one of my students had run off with the video store guy. "Of course," I backpedaled, "I'm sure there are some that are quite nice and faithful."

Santiago stared at me for a moment. Oh, no, I thought, I have grossly offended him. Stacey and I will be banished from the pool. We will spend the rest of the evening being attacked by *grillos* in our room.

But the stare soon became a smile, and the smile a laugh, and the laugh a guffaw. "Har, har, har," he bellowed, slapping the pool deck with his hand. Beneath the surface of the water, his belly shook. Enrique was smiling too. Linda wasn't smiling exactly, but she didn't look offended either. I was relieved they weren't angry, but I was confused about why he was laughing so hard. Had I misspoken? Or mangled something terribly in translation?

Santiago wiped a few tears from his face. "Most aren't faithful?" he spit out between fits of laughter, his face contorted and purple. "Most aren't faithful? *Pues, chica*, there isn't a single faithful man in all of Ecuador!"

To my astonishment, his wife did not dispute this. Presumably, he was included in "all of the men in Ecuador," but she didn't look the slightest bit angry or surprised or even irritated. She just nodded calmly, as if she were agreeing with him that it was sunny.

92

When he finally stopped laughing ten minutes later, he turned to me and said, "So would you be interested in marrying Enrique?"

I shook my head. "I'm sorry."

"Well I had to at least try," he said. "After all, he is my little brother."

An hour later, we were in the heat of battle. *Grillos* streamed into our room, crouching by the bathroom sink and pouncing each time we reached for the soap, as if instinctively knowing we would be caught off guard. They hid in our shoes, our luggage, our clothes. They tickled our arm hair with their antennas and raced up our calves. Every time we thought we had gotten the last *grillo* out of our room, another would pop up.

"I've had it," I finally said. "I am going to hunt down every last one of these little suckers and kill them. Stacey, help me move the beds."

We shoved the beds to the opposite wall and discovered that, just as I had surmised, more than a dozen *grillos* had been lurking beneath the beds. *Chirp, chirp.* "You are so busted," I said, as if I were talking to my wayward boys. "Stacey, blind them with the flashlight while I take them out."

"I am through being a nice animal lover," I grunted as I wielded my plastic Pepsi bottle like a mace. "I let you go, and what do you do? Come back and invite twelve of your friends." I smashed one little guy as he darted across the wall. "That's not nice. Not nice at all."

Stacey looked at me as if I were crazy, but I didn't care. This was war. With each thump of the Pepsi bottle, I let out a grunt of exertion. *Grillo* blood trickled down the walls; I felt like Rambo in a horror film about the plagues of Egypt.

When the last *grillo* had been killed, we settled into our beds and tucked in our mosquito nets. Victory was ours.

The next morning there were eyes everywhere in Puerto López. Oblong and lined with heavy black pigment, embedded in disconcertingly pink lumpy faces, they stared out at us like the kohl-ringed eyes of Egyptian mummies. It's just paper machê, I told myself each time as I hurried past. But even so I felt as though the eyes were following me. Some were propped against cinderblock walls, while others sat basking in the sun on unfinished second stories, inspecting jagged towers of rebar like concerned homeowners or huddling with their companion in what seemed to be an intimate chat. One couple was even nursing a couple of beers: a murky brown beer bottle was tucked in the crook of the black-haired gentleman's arm, nestled against his flannel shirt, while his red-haired wife clutched one to her ample bosom. She had what looked like a wart on the end of her nose and deep creases were gouged into her forehead. They were not a particularly attractive couple.

"Look," Stacey said. "They have names on their arms."

José Martínez Ayala, one arm read in shaky blue script. Sandra Obregón Díaz, red block letters announced below her green polka-dot shirtsleeve.

Further down the street, bespectacled Jorge was drinking a cup of coffee while plump Rosa was taking notes on a gigantic notepad filled with black squiggles. Samuel was wearing a suit and pointing his index finger angrily at us. He looked bloated and his mouth was twisted into a sneer.

"Maybe they are supposed to scare evil spirits away," I suggested as I felt myself come under the wrathful eye of Samuel. He certainly scared *me*.

Stacey seemed unconvinced. "But then why name them?"

"Maybe they are dead relatives. Dead scary relatives."

"Maybe."

We came to a small café on the beach and ordered the only breakfast you could order in Puerto López: two eggs, toast, hot chocolate, and juice. Every restaurant had the exact same menu; the only choice you had was scrambled or sunny-side up. "Do you know," I asked the waitress as she finished taking our order, "why there are life-sized dolls everywhere today? And why do they have names written on their arms?"

"They're for the bonfire tonight," she said. "Everyone makes one that looks like their boss and then hurls it on the fire at midnight to ring in the New Year."

"Don't their bosses mind?" I sputtered. It seemed like not the wisest course of action if one wanted a raise in the coming year.

She laughed. "I don't know. Maybe. But I don't think so. It's a tradition. Or maybe their bosses just don't come. Maybe they sit at home and watch TV. Or maybe they go on vacation somewhere else since they have money."

Somehow I thought it was the latter.

That evening, we tested my hypothesis in Salinas, a glitzy seaside resort a few hours south of Puerto López. It was filled with gleaming high-rises, chic bars, and stores hawking designer sunglasses and teeny bikinis. Glistening model-thin bodies wearing the latest fashions from Miami were stacked end-to-end on the sand; it seemed a world away from Puerto López and its pigs and *grillos*. The cheapest hotel room we could find was forty dollars—eight times what we had paid in Puerto López.

"All I see is Spiderman," Stacey observed as we sat on a concrete ledge overlooking the beach. Even from a hundred feet away, we could feel the inferno; our faces and torsos were hot to the touch. "Spiderman, Batman, Spiderman, Spiderman, some unidentified superhero, Britney Spears, Spiderman. I don't see anyone who remotely looks like a boss."

I didn't either. None of the figures wore suits or were fat or had wrinkles. They were all movie characters or celebrities, and no one needed to write their names on their arm. The Spiderman dolls even looked mass-produced, like something you would buy at Wal-Mart. "The thing is," I said, "these people probably *are* the bosses. They can't very well fling effigies of themselves on the fire."

"That's true. I guess for them this is more like Halloween."

The flames crept higher and higher, first twenty feet, then thirty, then forty into the air. About twenty minutes before midnight, the crowd began hurling the figures into the fire. It was a thrilling but terrifying spectacle: each time the fire would die down for a second, then shoot flames high into the air, sending burning embers flying every which way, as if someone had just poured gasoline on the fire. A couple times I thought the palm trees would catch on fire. But no one seemed the slightest bit concerned about fire safety: there were toddlers running around a few yards from the fire. There was no fire ring, and no safety barrier. I didn't even see any firemen on hand.

At midnight, the fireworks went off: a few quickly fizzled starbursts, a few pathetic bangs and pops. It was somewhat anticlimactic after all of the other pyrotechnics.

"Happy New Year!" we shouted, and another Spiderman went up in flames.

CHAPTER NINE

"So...did you go on your honeymoon with Paaaaaaablo?" Jefferson snickered and gave Juan a high-five while the rest of the class dissolved into laughter. I could tell he had been salivating over the prospect of being the first one to needle me about 'Pablo,' planning his delivery and timing for days, hoping to impress his classmates with his bravado.

"What? No 'how was your break, teacher'? 'Did you have a nice time on the coast?'"

"I don't need to ask. I *know* you had a good time...because you were with Pablo."

"Ooooooo....Paaaaaaaaablo," the rest of the class chimed in, as if on cue.

Darwin slugged Jefferson. "Don't forget she's married to *me*."

"Actually, I went to the coast with Stacey." Darwin beamed and the rest looked disappointed. I began writing long division problems on the chalkboard. "You've got ten minutes to do these problems. First one with all of them correct wins a sucker." Anything sweet was a great motivator, and I used it to my advantage. It was a trade-off: they got their sugar high—which conveniently kicked in just as Paul was taking over—and I recovered (some of) my sanity.

Biting their lips and furrowing their brows, they hunched over their desks in intense concentration. Conversation came to a halt, and pencils moved furiously over the pages. Occasionally they would make a mistake. Then they would curse under their breaths, grab a fistful of hair or smack their foreheads with the palms of their hands (as if they had just discovered a new property of quarks and

97

were about to run through the streets shouting "Eureka!"), and then rub out the error with unnatural violence, sometimes even ripping the paper in the process. They never crossed out an error. They insisted on eliminating all vestiges of error, extirpating them, purging them. With a single determined sweep of the hand, whole dust clouds of pink rubber shavings were suspended in the air. I think my class single-handedly supported an entire rubber plantation.

I loved these first few minutes of class, before they got bored, when they were totally absorbed in their work and eager to please. I could almost see the gears in their little brains turning, and the excitement of mastering something new and difficult—long division, just like the junior high school students!—was palpable.

The silence only lasted but a few moments. As soon as the first problem was finished, the hands went up. "Maureen! Maureen! Maureen! Maureen!" Each one called my name at least four times, and bounced up and down in his seat as if he had an urgent need to use the restroom. "I'm done with the first one! Did I get the right answer?" "Come check my answer!" "I raised my hand before Juan! Why do you always go to him first?" And so on, and so on. This was standard procedure. No matter how many times I tried to break them of the habit, they always insisted I check each problem as soon as they had finished. And in a strange way, that was their charm. They were tough and they were independent and they were street-smart, they were wise beyond their years, they shouldered heavy financial responsibilities for their families at a tender young age, and yet they were also insecure, hyperactive teenage boys in need of constant reassurance and attention. There was something almost puppy-like about them: all they wanted was to be patted on the head and told they had done a good job.

Suddenly there was an unexpected yelp. "My Atari!" Raúl wailed. "It's gone. Someone stole it!" He shot the class an accusatory glance and began to sweat. "I have to get it back! It's my brother's and he'll kill me if I don't give it back!"

"Okay, everyone stand up and open your backpacks." I knew the drill, having done it twice before. The first time, I had searched all of the backpacks before a witness admitted to seeing one of the boys throw a sweatshirt out the window; I had sent an emissary to recover the sweatshirt, and order was restored. The second time, I had been subbing for a class of all girls, and had had to search down to their socks, but had never recovered the three dollars reportedly stolen. Don Rodrigo ended up making each of the girls pay the aggrieved party a dime, hoping this would convince one of the girls to squeal, but no one ever came forward.

They stood next to their desks and unzipped their backpacks for my inspection. I fingered every nook and cranny, searching each boy's face as I did so for the slightest flinch or smile or glance that betrayed an ounce of guilt. They all had the poker face down pat. When I had inspected the last backpack and found nothing, I was at a loss, with no clear idea how to proceed. The windows were shut today, so that was not an option.

"He must have had an accomplice," Juan helpfully suggested. "While you inspected one kid's backpack, the other had it, and vice versa."

"Maybe it's in his pants," Jefferson piped up and then, true to form, added with a sly smile, "Are you going to strip search us?"

"Maureen wouldn't do that," Raúl said. The class and I stared each other down. It was a challenge, and they were counting on my prudishness to protect the offender in their midst.

I walked slowly towards the door, my mind made up. Without taking my eyes off the class, I opened the door behind me and roared, "INSPECTOR!"

The Inspector came running from his office. "How can I help you, Señorita?"

"Someone stole Raúl's Atari. I need your help searching the boys."

"*Claro, claro,*" the Inspector said, always the gentleman, as if this were a most usual request. He berated Raúl for bringing an Atari to school in the first place, ranted about how he should give the money to his mother instead for groceries, and then proceeded to take each boy aside, ask him to stand against the wall, and pat him down, while I stood in the corner of the room and watched the other boys with eagle eyes, ready to pounce at the first sign of collusion.

The search dragged on, with each boy loudly protesting his innocence. "It's not my fault if he lost his game," Juan grumbled.

"He probably didn't even bring it to school in the first place." Jefferson shot Raúl a contemptuous look and, having received the all-clear from the Inspector, swaggered back to his seat like P. Diddy beating a murder rap.

The Inspector pointed at Darwin. "You're next."

Darwin rose, his usual toothy grin replaced by the pout of the falsely accused, and took a step towards the Inspector. There was a soft thud, and the Atari slid out of his pants leg onto the floor. I was incredulous. Jefferson had been right—it *was* in someone's pants.

"Thief!" the Inspector roared.

"I didn't do it! I didn't! I swear! I was framed! Someone put it there!"

I couldn't believe his audacity. "Someone put it in your pants??"

"Yes!"

"And you didn't notice?"

"No, I—"

"You didn't notice a large, square, plastic object in your pants?" These kids will lie about anything, I thought. They must think I am really dumb.

The Inspector went over to Darwin, grabbed hold of his earlobe, and pulled him out the door, down the hall, and into his office. The door slammed shut so hard the whole wing of the building shook.

I leaned against the chalkboard and put a hand to my throbbing head. Paul walked in. "Rough day, huh?"

"They're all yours."

I sentenced Darwin to the closest thing to hard labor in a Siberian gulag that I could come up with: a whole week of bathroom duty, during the middle of the day for maximum humiliation, supervised by Madre Kathy. After he had completed his sentence, he was to write a letter of apology to me and to Raúl, and ask me to let him back into class. I felt pretty generous, all things considered, especially since his parents offered to give him a beating he would never forget. I asked them to please desist and resolved to handle all further discipline problems without parental input.

At the end of the week, a repentant Darwin stood in the doorway of my classroom, letter in hand. Without saying a word, I took it and examined it. It looked like a kindergartener had written it, with huge shaky block letters, absolutely atrocious spelling, and no punctuation. The parts I could decipher were sufficiently contrite, however. He looked up at me tearfully. "Please, please, Maureen, let me back in class."

"Why should I?"

"I don't know, I—I want to learn. I—I—"

"What?"

"I want to do better. I know I screwed up, but I want to try and behave."

"You need to apologize to Raúl."

"I know."

"You need to stop causing me problems."

"I know. I'm sorry."

"One more time and you're out. You're out of the Center for good. Do you understand?"

He nodded slowly, miserably.

"Good. Have a seat. And one more thing: I want you here every day for tutoring before class. I don't want you getting in trouble before class, and you need to improve your grades."

The rest of the class soon arrived. Darwin sat glumly in his seat. For once, he looked truly chastised. Then he raised his hand. I sighed and called on him, expecting some sort of smart-aleck request. "Maureen, could I please sit up front? I think it would be easier…for me to behave."

I waved him up to an empty desk in the front row, relieved. He turned to Raúl and said, "I'm sorry I stole your game." Then he sat down, took out two freshly sharpened pencils and a notebook and stared intently at the board.

I felt as though I had a new student in class, and perhaps I did.

Fresh from my success molding (at least temporarily) Darwin into a model student and citizen, I launched into an ambitious attempt to give my ninth graders a little bit of culture.

Don Rodrigo was not impressed. "You want my secretaries to make photocopies of—of—eleventh-century Spanish *poems?*" he sputtered.

"Eleventh-century Spanish *epic* poems. As you may recall, the Ecuadorian Education Department's required curriculum includes epic poetry. It will be on the test required for graduation."

"But that is just a formality. Every year they threaten to fail our students, and every year they pass all of them, whether they know anything or not. Maureen, a vegetable could pass!"

"But what if this year is different? Shouldn't they at least be somewhat prepared?" I persisted. "And besides, I'm only having them read two pages of excerpts. How bad can it be?"

"Bad! And useless," he retorted, clearly exasperated with me and what he no doubt perceived as my naïve, newfangled, utopian ideas. I think he was particularly disturbed by the image of his macho auto mechanic students suddenly sprouting bloomers and becoming wandering troubadour pansies. Poetry did not fit into Don Rodrigo's Dickensian worldview: the best possible outcome, as far as he was concerned, was that they devoted every bit of their limited mental capacity to learning a trade; anything that detracted from this goal was superfluous. In many ways, he had a point, but sometimes it seemed that he—and the Madres and the Padre—took it a bit far. "Why don't you have them read a mechanic's manual? Or sewing instructions? These kids have no use for poetry, and they won't understand a single word."

"I think you underestimate them. *El Mío Cid* is about conflict and love, two things they understand. And I will help them understand all of the hard words. We'll learn to use the dictionary. It will be a growth experience."

"This is nuts," he said softly, but I could tell that he had run out of arguments.

The next day I had sixty copies on my desk.

The kids eyed me suspiciously as I passed out dictionaries. "Are we going to have to actually use these?" one of my troublemakers asked.

"Absolutely," I said in my best cheery Mary Poppins voice. "It will be a great experience. We are all going to work together to expand our vocabulary. Won't that be fun?"

"No."

I ignored him and pretended I didn't see everyone else rolling their eyes and shifting uncomfortably in their seats. "Today we are going to begin a unit on epic poetry and we are going to begin to read part of the most famous epic poem ever written in the Spanish language, *El Mío Cid*."

The boys looked even more depressed. "Don't worry," I chirped like a deranged Pollyanna who had wandered into a prison camp, "the hero El Cid falls in love with a hot chick and kills a whole bunch of bad guys in a bloody battle." I paused for dramatic effect. "Now, *El Mío Cid* takes place in the eleventh century in Spain." They looked at me blankly. "Who knows where Spain is?" I held up a blank map of Europe. "Can someone come up here and show me where Spain is?"

One boy swaggered to the front and put his hand on England. "No, that's *Gran Bretaña*," I said gently. "Okay, somebody else then. Maybe somebody who has family in Spain."

One-quarter of the population of Ecuador had left the country in the last decade—one of the largest mass migrations in history on a per capita basis—and most of these emigrants had gone to Spain or Italy. Surely one of the students had a relative in Spain and was curious enough to have found out where it was.

One of the beauty school students shyly raised her hand and came to the front of the room. She put her finger on Italy and I shook my head. She bit her lip and shuffled back to her seat.

"Africa!" someone shouted out.

"Asia!"

"Antarctica?"

I sighed deeply and traced my finger around Spain's borders. "This is Spain. This is where a lot of your relatives live now and where some of your ancestors came from."

They looked confused. One of the girls in the front row raised her hand. "What language do they speak there?"

Once we had sorted out that Spain was in Europe, that the Spanish actually *spoke* Spanish, and that Spain had not only conquered the Inca Empire (of which Ecuador had been a part) but also helped people it, everything went a whole lot smoother. Whenever they didn't understand a word—which is to say frequently, about once every line of poetry—they would frown and begin to flip though the dictionary. They would start at "A" and then go through each letter until they found the first letter of the word. Then they would recite the alphabet out loud to find out where the second letter of the word was in relation to the other letters, since they did not instinctively know that "n" was before "p" unless they recited the whole alphabet from the beginning. Before long it would sound as if the students were singing a round of the alphabet song. Then finally someone would find the word and raise his or her hand triumphantly. Then the process of deciphering the definition would begin. This whole process could take five minutes or more.

After reading and more or less comprehending four lines, we would stop, and if possible, reenact what had just happened. I picked the class's most dramatic couple—Patricio and Elena, who were always in the midst of either a dramatic break-up or a lovey-dovey reconciliation period—to play El Cid and his wife Ximena, which had the whole class hooting. When it came time to reenact the battle scenes, I outfitted a few of the toughest guys with cardboard tubes and taught them how to fence. We also simulated horseback riding, which they had never seen except on TV.

Five or six class periods later, we had read a whole page and a half of the poem and contrary to Don Rodrigo's dire prediction, almost everyone understood what it was about. They sat enraptured, watching Charlton Heston romance Elizabeth Taylor, then ride off into the sunset to slay a whole army of Moors, in a badly-dubbed grainy movie version of the poem. The raven, a portent of malevolent things to come, alighted on Elizabeth Taylor's shoulder and I shrieked, "The raven! See? It's the raven we read about in the poem," and they looked at me like I had lost my marbles.

I remembered that look: my classmates and I had given all of our eccentric language arts teachers the same one. And now, I realized, I was that teacher.

CHAPTER TEN

By the end of January, love was in the air. Florid love poems replaced stilted paragraphs in the ninth-graders' journals, and a flurry of love notes (misspelled, of course) were furtively passed around the room. Attention spans were at an all-time low. Had reading *El Cid* inspired them to try their own hand at courtly love? Was it the impending Valentine's Day? Or was it just restlessness brought on by the onset of the rainy season?

"Can't you fall in love when you're not in class?" I asked, exasperated, as I intercepted yet another note. It was written in bubble gum pink ink, with little hearts dotting the "i"s, and signed *"con muchisisisísimo amor,"* because apparently loving Miguel very, very much wasn't enough. She loved him very, very, very, very much, and she wanted him to know.

"No, Maureen," one of my beauty students explained. "We don't ever see each other outside of class. After class, we have to go home. On the weekends, we stay at home. Class is where we have our relationships."

"Oh, I thought class was where you learned."

She shook her head solemnly. Apparently she thought *I* had a lot to learn.

Frustrated as I was with their short attention spans, I had to admit that I felt a bit sorry for them. They never had the chance to interact the way American teenagers did. Their families were spread out in shantytowns all across the valley; it took some of them up to an hour and half each way to come to school. They couldn't walk to each other's houses, and they certainly didn't have cars. They didn't have telephones so there was no way to annoy their parents by

105

spending all night gabbing with their girlfriends. They didn't even have the bus fare to go see a friend on a Saturday.

To rectify the problem, I decided to organize a junior high dance for Valentine's Day. It was pretty comic, really, considering that I had been too shy and too nerdy to attend a single dance when I was in high school; I spent the night of my Prom making cookies with a few of the other Prom rejects. But suddenly I felt that this was a terrific idea. I was enthused. I was gung-ho. I was going to make this a night to remember, no matter what.

When I told Madre Kathy about my idea, however, she was a bit less enthused. "Go ahead, organize a dance," she said. "It's one big headache." She laughed, but not because she thought there was anything funny about it. "But don't expect any help from us. And only kids without disciplinary problems can attend, and the chaperones must check Center I.D.'s at the door and make sure no alcohol is brought in." She suggested I hire Roberto, the D.J. from the *quinceañera*, for the dance.

I ran into Lucía, Roberto's wife, on the playground a few days later. She was dark and plain, a small woman even by Ecuadorian standards, with world-weary eyes and a perpetual look of dejection. Her lips were always set in a thin, determined line, as if she were afraid that if she opened her mouth to speak, she would unleash a litany of complaints about the great gulf between her hardscrabble life and the more grandiose lifestyle to which status as the Madre's quasi-adopted child—Lucía had been an orphan—and marriage to Roberto should have entitled her. She seemed terrified of anyone seeing her vulnerabilities and disappointments, infinitely more comfortable regarding the world behind a deceptively vacant stare. This stare was her protector. It shielded her from seeing that anyone had more or better than she, and most of all, it masked her insecurities and her intense fear that people were laughing at her folly in marrying Roberto and actually believing that he, the most eligible bachelor at the Center, had eyes only for her. Only in her late twenties, she seemed old somehow. However purposefully she walked, I always had the impression that she had one foot in the grave, and was just biding her time in this god-forsaken corner of the planet until called home to rest at last.

She looked away from me, her gaze scanning the vast expanse of dirt and sand that stretched before us, broken only by a graceful ancient oak, as I made my request. Nodding slowly, she replied in a monotone, "I'll check with Roberto tonight. That should be fine." Then she hurried away.

The next day she approached me in the hallway and confirmed that Roberto would provide the music. "It's the fifteenth, right?"

"Right. How much will he charge?"

"Forty dollars."

"*Cuarenta?*" I was incredulous—that was almost half a month's rent.

"*Cuarenta,*" she repeated, firmly. "He provides his own transportation. That's included."

"But it's for the Center," I pleaded. It seemed ridiculous for someone raised in the Center to bilk us so.

"Usually it's seventy," she said. "Forty for you." Her lips set again in a thin, determined line, and I knew no further negotiation was possible.

When I announced the Valentine's Day dance to my ninth-graders, they were positively jubilant. "Are we going to have a D.J.?" one of the beauty girls asked.

"*Sí.*"

"What about popcorn? Last year they made popcorn."

"We'll see about that."

"Are you going to dance, Maureen?" one of the mechanics boys asked.

"Of course."

"We need decorations!"

"Big hearts…"

"…and streamers!"

I knew I needed to draw the line. "Listen, I am getting a D.J. and bringing beverages. *You* can make the decorations. We will therefore have our first Dance Committee meeting tonight at seven. I'll provide the materials, you provide the labor." And with that, I dismissed the class and headed off to the art supply room.

At seven, I founded myself seated around a table in the cafeteria with crayons, construction paper, scissors, tape, glue, glitter, and seven boys, most of them mechanics. "What happened to the girls?"

They shrugged. "The girls always say they're coming and then don't show up. They're so unreliable. But don't worry, Maureen, you can count on us."

They hunched over the table, the sleeves on their hand-me-downs reaching halfway up to their elbows, tracing big misshapen hearts on pink and red construction paper. The first few ended up looking like distended chicken livers. "Here," I said, feeling like my kindergarten teacher, "try this." I folded a piece of construction paper in half and traced half of a heart, cut it, and unfolded the more or less symmetric shape.

They looked at me as if I had just performed open heart surgery. "*Chévere.*" With great industriousness, they set about adopting my technique.

This scene repeated itself every day at seven. A core group of boys would arrive, plunk themselves down, and set to work creating posters and paper hearts. They would chew their lips anxiously as they outlined all kinds of sappy phrases in glue, then liberally pour on the glitter, and shake off the excess very carefully. A few girls would saunter over occasionally, staying just long enough to inspect the boys' handiwork before flitting off again to rejoin their clique of whispering, gossiping, giggling friends.

Zach walked past during one of these sessions. He tried to look serious as he inspected their work, but I could tell he was on the verge of laughter. "I love it," he said. "You've got all of your tough guys cutting out little pink hearts."

He stood and chatted for a moment, then was dragged away by a demanding pre-schooler. All eyes turned toward me. "What did he say? What did he say?" they asked excitedly.

"He says you're all very artistic," I lied. They beamed and kept working.

Madre Kathy came by, looking displeased. "You've got a big problem."

"I do?"

"Yep."

"What is it?"

"I talked to Roberto today. I mentioned the dance, and he acted like he knew nothing about it."

How could that be? The dance was just a week away and Lucía had promised. I had even agreed to pay Roberto the full forty dollars. "But I told Lucía and she said—"

"You need to talk to him," she said brusquely. "And probably get yourself a new D.J."

Roberto and Lucía eluded me for two days until I finally spotted Lucía coming out of Madre's office. "What is this I hear about Roberto not being available for the Valentine's Day dance?" I snapped.

"He has another engagement," she said in her characteristic monotone, her vacant stare affixed on her face, without the slightest embarrassment, as if she hadn't assured me a few weeks ago that they had discussed it and he was free.

"You told me he would do the dance."

She looked at me passively, pretending not to understand why I was peeved.

"Why did you tell me he was available if he wasn't?"

She shrugged. "I thought he was."

"But he isn't."

"Right."

I felt like punching her, but instead, without another word, I stomped right past her, down the steps, across the muddy field, and into the Center's warehouse, a musty, poorly-lit enclosed concrete slab the size of a football field jammed with odd assortments of supplies from well-meaning but often clueless American donors and the occasional multinational corporation. The Madres managed to find a use for everything, though, and that was the beauty of the warehouse. "*Don Mateo*," I said, with due deference, as a tall, gaunt man on the cusp of old age, with skin black as coal, limped towards me. His tattered mud-colored trousers hung awkwardly on his rail-thin frame, and his short-sleeved shirt, once white, now beige, hung open at the neck.

"*Señorita*," he said, returning the deference and greeting me with a brief air kiss on each cheek. He was at once humble, yet dignified. His weather-beaten skin hinted of long hot days toiling in the fields and his eyes had the piercing quality of one who has seen much and forgotten little, but unlike Lucía, he radiated a contented sort of resignation to his lot in life and gratitude and joy for the small blessings that had come his way.

"Yo soy la voluntaria Maureen," I said, by way of introduction. "I am the one organizing the Valentine's Day dance."

He smiled and the skin around his eyes crinkled up like folds on an elephant's skin. "Ah, yes, the dance. I've been hearing a lot about that."

"I've been told that in your neighborhood, there is a D.J. who graduated from the Center, and that you could take me to him."

He bowed slightly. "Of course. It would be my pleasure. Anything for the Center. The Center has taught me so much, given me so much…" He trailed off as he took me gently by the arm and led me to the bus stop, where we waited in the late afternoon sunshine. When the bus arrived, Don Mateo paid my fare before I could protest and then limped to a bench in the rear. He proudly pointed out various landmarks and Center members' homes as the bus creaked up the dusty hills dotted with spindly poplars and bright, boxy homes and businesses. At one point, though, he saddened. "Unfortunately, as wonderful as this neighborhood is, it's not safe. You should never come here unless you are accompanied by a Center member. Remember that."

We alighted near the end of the route, on a dusty dirt lane identical to all of the other dusty dirt lanes we had passed. An emaciated dog frothing at the mouth trailed us, shoulders hunched forward, like a wolf; I watched him warily out of the corner of my eye and prayed that my rabies vaccination was up to date. We passed a bony boy, about ten, joyriding on a rusted-out bicycle, and a couple of women laden with groceries. Everyone was an impenetrable shade of black and almost everyone was very thin. The parents and grandparents of these people had been laborers in the plantations of the Chota Valley to the north, or had decided to move inland from the swampy, mosquito-infested fishing communities and banana plantations of the coast in search of a better life—one that had evidently not materialized (or so I thought)—in Quito. Now their children inhabited this tiny island of Africa marooned among a sea of indigenous highlanders who, at best, considered them a race apart, and at worst, treated them with contempt.

Don Mateo paused at the door of a white two-story house, unusual in this neighborhood, and knocked. A muffled voice called out suspiciously, "Who is it?"

"Mateo."

The door swung wide open. *"Don Mateo!"* a large black woman exclaimed, throwing open the door. She wore a muumuu, or something like it, so very different from the conservative and relatively colorless outfits of indigenous Ecuadorian women, with their white lacy blouses and long black skirts. Not even asking who I was, she ushered us inside and motioned for us to sit on the couch, which was upholstered with a gaudy floral print and covered with protective vinyl sheeting.

Don Mateo explained my predicament and she became most businesslike. "What day did you say it was? What time? How much were you going to pay? What kind of music do you want?" She noted every detail down on a notepad. Unlike most of the Ecuadorian adults I knew, she wrote quickly and without hesitation. I wish my kids could write like that, I thought. "Is that it?" she finally asked.

"I think so."

"Well," she said triumphantly, "I'm quite sure my Andrés is just the man you need. He'll be home later this evening and I'll have him call you. We have a phone, you know. Almost no one in this neighborhood has a phone, but we do. The Center taught us to work hard and to save." She paused. "My Andrés just loves the Center, so I am sure that if he is available, he would be very happy to do this. He's a graduate, you know. So am I. They taught me how to read."

We stood up and shook hands firmly. With our business deal concluded, Don Mateo and I paraded back down the street, starving dog and bike-happy child still in tow. I breathed a sigh of relief.

The dance did not unfold as I expected. Hermano Paco was half an hour late in bringing Andrés and his equipment, so I spent the first thirty minutes chewing my nails and asking the volunteers setting up with me if they could sing. In between these near-meltdowns, I supervised my Dance Committee as they draped streamers across the overhead beams in the covered patio and dangled glittery hearts from the ceiling. "Oh, Maureen, it looks so beautiful," one of the girls sighed.

In all honesty, it didn't. The decorations were gaudy and mismatched and obviously homemade, and even if they hadn't been, it's hard to spruce up gray concrete. To me, it looked like an elementary school hallway in which student artwork, no matter how dreadful, is proudly displayed, and that's essentially what it was. But still, I thought, I'm glad *they* think it's beautiful. Beauty is in the eye of the beholder, anyway.

Andrés finally arrived. His equipment was more impressive than I had expected, and he was tall, slender, and good-looking. He had a serious expression, and he wore an expensive new athletic warm-up suit. While he tested the sound system, he grooved in place. The booming Dominican rap music was incomprehensible to me, but Andrés seemed entranced.

At six, the doors officially opened. I had expected a crowd within minutes, but all I got was a trickle, and not a very lively trickle at that. Everyone stood against the wall, as if glued there by centrifugal force. The boys were on one side, the girls on the other. Most were dressed in one of the only two or three outfits they had—outfits we volunteers saw so often that we began to identify children by the clothes they wore. "Oh, you don't know which one Pedrito is?" one of the volunteers would say. "He's the one with the red pants and the purple striped shirt." Then the other volunteer would nod, the name and the face (or clothing, as it were) now matched.

A few of the kids bent their knees ever so slightly in time to the music, as if to suggest that maybe, maybe they could be enticed to dance if the right person came along. Andrés looked depressed.

Zach and I decided to walk the wallflower wall: I took the boys' side of the room, and he took the girls'. I spotted Raúl and grabbed his wrist, pulling him towards the center of the dance floor. "Noooooooooo, Maureen," he wailed, digging his feet into the floor and clawing at the cinderblock wall behind him with his free hand. The boys around him clutched each other for support. "I can't dance. Maybe later. Not now. Later. I promise!"

I let go for an instant and the whole group fled into the boys' bathroom, where they apparently hoped to be out of reach. You'd have thought we were the Gestapo. I had to give them plaudits for their strategy, though, since the bathroom's stench was so overpowering that none of the male volunteers were willing to go in there to root them out. Occasionally the boys in the bathroom would half-emerge from their hide-out and loiter in the doorway, keenly observing the scene and listening to the music. Then, as soon as I would take a step towards them, they would scatter back into the interior of their den and intimate that one of them was about to use the urinals, at which point I had no choice to retreat. I felt as though I were in some kind of bizarre game of tag.

"We're going to have to start dancing ourselves," Zach muttered. He took me by the arm, motioned for Stacey and Paul to join us, and headed into the middle of the patio. There the four of us stood, smiling sheepishly, nodding our heads in time (sort of) with the music, trying to catch the beat, and painfully aware of just how ridiculous we looked.

We took our first tentative salsa steps, smiling our big plastic isn't-this-fun-kids smiles, trying to ignore the hundred little eyes boring into our backsides. I was normally a horrible dancer, but now, knowing that I was the center of attention, I just got worse. Every time Zach turned me, I somehow let go of his hand. I turned overly abruptly, as though I were afraid that a slow, measured turn was inappropriate in this setting, as if it were too intimate or too sexy (as if I could ever be too sexy, especially in a sweaty institutional-looking patio). Half the time I crashed into him nearly head-on as I finished the turn, or stomped on his foot, after which I turned bright red, apologized profusely, and stared assiduously at the floor before remembering that I was a teacher on a mission, rather than a nervous schoolgirl, and resolutely faced my onlookers, chin up, plastic smile plastered on once more.

After enduring one whole song, we split up to try to attract new—student—dance partners. Once again, the kids shrieked, clawed the wall, dropped to their knees in desperate supplication, or clutched pillars or bystanders' waists or knees or ankles, anything at all, to avoid being pried into the circle, as if we were tornados threatening to whisk them away, never to return to the comforting anonymity of the wallflower ring. I could not comprehend how children who had been so ecstatic about the prospect of a dance could be so afraid to actually dance. "But dancing is what you do at a dance," I explained, half-irritated, to one of my resisters.

"Everyone dances," he corrected me, "but not until the end. Not until everyone else does."

"But if no one starts, then no one can join in. Then the dance ends with no one dancing."

He shrugged and fled to the boys' bathroom.

Ten minutes later, we were still alone. Zach walked over to the D.J. stand, whispered conspiratorially in Andrés's ear for a long time, and then took hold of the mike. *"Vamos a tener un concurso de baile!"* he announced, as if he were a game show host. The kids stared at him. A few shook their heads back and forth vigorously. He carefully explained that the contest was to last one song, and that the winners would receive free movie tickets. Free, of course, meant paid for by the volunteers on our nonexistent salaries.

Andrés chose a slow song, and one lone couple shyly stepped onto the floor. They swayed this way and that, staring at the floor. I was sure that they would win by default, but soon, to my surprise, a second couple joined them, then a third. By the end of the song, roughly a fifth of the students were dancing.

"What a relief," I said to Zach as we stood by the punch bowl. I was so happy to no longer be the center of attention.

"Andrés is actually pretty good," Zach said. "Better than Roberto, probably. And so far he hasn't tried to pick up any of the girls."

"Also a relief."

We went out on the dance floor and danced a few songs. I danced with Paul and Stacey and even Darwin. "This is an awesome dance," he yelled as we jolted up and down like Mexican jumping beans. He didn't know how to salsa; his version of dancing was to jump up and down as frenetically as possible.

When the dance came to a close an hour later, I didn't have to ask for help cleaning up. Wordlessly, automatically, my ninth-graders pushed the tables back into position, swept the floor, threw out the garbage, and took down the decorations. They left it just as they had found it, a forlorn and humble patio, and yet somehow, as they drifted off to their homes, it retained a certain magic quality, a certain sparkle, a hint of promise of the future.

CHAPTER ELEVEN

The rainy season was cold and dreary. Mornings were the worst: waking to an eerie gray half-light, reluctantly swinging my goose-pimpled legs out from under the mounds of covers, cringing as my feet brushed the ice-cold floor tiles, and then shivering uncontrollably as I waited for the shower to heat up. Sometimes I distracted myself from the cold by counting my ribs in the mirror; frequent illnesses and the surprisingly aerobic demands of teaching had taken their toll and I could now see every rib, even without sucking in my stomach. More often than not, I eventually gave up on the shower. It was hardly ever warmer than tepid, and sometimes it was downright frigid. Our water was solar-heated and without the sun, well, it didn't really get heated. It occurred to me, of course, that in my students' homes, every day—whether in the rainy season or not—was a cold shower day, and that instead of keeping warm at night with fluffy blankets, they had to make do by huddling with parents, siblings, and even the family's animals, but even so, it was hard to bear. I was more of a prima donna than I thought.

The silver lining was that the inclement weather provided an excuse for my *nivelación* students to come and see me before class, whether to get some extra help or just to chat. "It's raining too much to play *fútbol,*" Edison would explain as he sauntered into the classroom forty-five minutes early and perched on top of a desk. Usually I knew for a fact that there were twenty boys toughing it out on the muddy field in what was really only a steady drizzle, but I would respectfully say nothing. I didn't want to chip away at his tough façade. "You'll be happy to know," he would then say as he leaned back on the desk, "that Liga won on Sunday." Or if they lost, he would shake his head sorrowfully and pat me on the back as if comforting me, "I know you're upset that Liga lost." I would try my best to look appropriately distraught. Ever since Juan had made it known that I claimed to be a Liga fan, Edison took it upon himself to update me at least once a week on Liga's standing. It seemed to me that Paul would be a much better person for Edison to talk *fútbol* with, but since Paul still insisted Edison was psychotic and Edison thought Paul hated him, I got the update instead.

Darwin, Jefferson, and Raúl would usually burst in a few minutes later. "Can we play 'Hangman' again?" they would plead as if I really would turn down an opportunity to trick them into doing math problems.

"Remember, I'm your *marido*," Darwin would say, shooting me one of his toothy grins. "You're going to let me win, right?"

"Wrong."

If Edison didn't think I was paying enough attention to him, he would poke my arm. One day he announced that he wanted to be like Michael Jordan when he grew up. "How tall do you have to be to be an American basketball player?" he asked nonchalantly as he tapped his cheek. *Thwap, thwap.* I could tell that secretly, however, he was very interested in my answer.

"Really, really tall," I said.

"As tall as you?"

I laughed. On my driver's license, I claimed to be five-foot-five, but even that was with shoes on. "No, a lot taller than I am."

Initially, Juan had also been a regular, but as the rainy season dragged on, I saw him less and less frequently before class. And then I began to see him less and less frequently in class. "What's going on with Juan?" I asked Edison one day before class.

Edison shrugged. *Thwap, thwap.*

"He has a girlfriend," Jefferson piped up and then added in a hushed voice, "An older woman."

"How much older?"

"*Diecisiete*," he whispered and looked very impressed. I could see why. Juan was only fourteen, so for a seventeen-year-old to pay attention to him certainly was a big deal.

When Juan finally made an appearance a few days later, I asked him about his new girlfriend. "Which one?" he asked. "I have so many, Maureen," he crowed as he gave me a bone-crushing handshake and then twisted my arm behind my back, laughing. The handshake was kind of a joke between us, but lately it had become something more: an assertion of his authority and proof of his ever-increasing strength. We're friends, the handshake said, but don't get too comfortable. I am strong, and I am in charge. He was wearing a new red sweater, new blue jeans, and new sneakers, and I suddenly realized how much he had changed since the beginning of the year. He stood taller and more confidently, he dressed better, he was healthier-looking and better fed, he was more assertive and articulate. His grip was stronger and his voice was deeper. He always looked everyone straight in the eye, and often there was a glimmer of laughter in his eyes. In many ways, his parents' move to the city has proved fortuitous. And yet in his cocky response, I also glimpsed what had been lost: his innocence, his shy humility, his deference to authority, and the seriousness with which he had once approached his studies. In some ways, I missed the old Juan, the respectful and mysterious Juan who wore tattered old sweaters and would never have thought of himself as a ladies' man. But I knew that I missed someone who no longer existed. What had been lost could not be regained, and that was probably as it should be.

On these rainy late afternoons, Don Rodrigo would often stop by. He would hover discreetly in the doorway, his muscular forearms crossed over his broad chest. From time to time, he would nod approvingly. "*Muy bien*, Maureen," he would say in his gravelly voice, with just a hint of a smile. "*Muy, muy bien.*" Then he would lock eyes with me, silently pump his fist (thereby reminding me to keep on using the "*mano dura*"), and continue on down the hallway.

Don Rodrigo had become a most unlikely fan.

It was during a hailstorm that I discovered just what a softie Edison really was. It was a Thursday and I was running late. Past the eucalyptus tree I sprinted, covering my head with my hands. *Ping, ping.* Hundreds of little white pellets battered my hands and obscured the path before me, bouncing off the pavement and ricocheting off the playground equipment. My hands stung. I bounded up the path and plodded across the field, ankle-deep in reddish-brown mud, slipping and sliding as I went. Finally, I

117

thought, as I reached the covered passageway in front of the cafeteria, I can stop and catch my breath.

I leaned my drenched body against the open doorway of the cafeteria. It felt so good to be out of the driving rain, the wind, and the hail. I waved to a couple of girls who were busy coloring, and I greeted a couple of the parents as they walked in and out, hauling vegetables for the evening meal. And then, in the corner, I saw Edison.

He was not the sullen, non-responsive Edison I knew at the beginning of the year, or even the somewhat calmer, gentler—but still tough—Edison that I had seen glimpses of lately. No, this Edison was ebullient, spontaneous, carefree, and silly. There was nothing tough about him. He was not punching anyone. He was not flinging rubber bands. He was not even carving his initials or tapping his cheek or blowing bubbles.

He was playing with two little girls.

One was about eight, a scrawny little girl in a faded blue T-shirt. The other was perhaps ten, with two lopsided pigtails and a swollen belly poking out from under an orange blouse. The younger girl was perched on Edison's back, her hands clasped tightly around his neck and her legs wrapped around his stomach, while Edison twirled the older girl around in a circle. "Edison," the older girl shrieked, delighted. "EDISON!"

Soon the three of them were engaged in a spirited game of tag. I watched in amazement as Edison patiently covered his eyes and counted to ten and then began to chase his companions, rather slowly, as they darted between pillars. He clearly wasn't trying to win.

I decided to go over and say hello. As I approached, however, I saw that there was something horribly wrong with the girls' faces. Lopsided and bruised, scabs covered their cheeks, their foreheads, their chins, and even their lips. One of the girl's ears was partly ripped from her body and an oozing red sore ran the length of her earlobe, along her hairline. And yet at that moment they looked so very happy.

"*Hola*, Edison," I said. "Are these your friends?"

"*No, son mis hermanas*," he said proudly. I introduced myself to his sisters and we greeted each other with the customary kiss on the cheek. The older one told me her name was Josefa, but the other one said nothing at all. "She's mute," Edison explained in a low voice.

In class that day, I was distracted. I kept looking over at Edison, searching for clues about his sisters. Why did they have so many bruises? Why was the younger one mute? And was there a connection between his sisters' condition and Edison's three-inch scar?

In search of answers, I sought out Susana, the Spanish-teacher-turned-nun who answered all of my most vexing Spanish grammar questions and had served as a sounding board for me all year. "Yes, I know that family well," she said thoughtfully as I described my encounter. She wrinkled her forehead and shook her head slowly from side to side. "It's very tragic. The stepfather is very abusive and the mother is an alcoholic. We believe the younger girl suffered some kind of sexual trauma. There appears to be no physical reason that she is unable to talk, but as long as I have been here she has been mute."

Then Susana told me something that startled me: she had conducted a comprehensive survey of the girls at the Center for her doctoral dissertation in psychology. I was embarrassed to admit I didn't even know that she was a graduate student.

"Well, I don't talk about it too much," Susana explained. "The findings were a bit depressing."

"And the findings were...?"

"A quarter of our girls admitted to having been sexually abused by a male relative living in their household. And it's not just stepfathers and stepbrothers. Sometimes it's their own flesh and blood, their own brothers and fathers."

When I repeated that to Jeannie later that night, she didn't seem all that surprised. "I heard that one of the junior high girls was raped by her father," she reported. She hopped up, crossed the room to raid her secret stash of Reese's peanut butter cups—her mom had sent her hundreds, as if in anticipation of a worldwide peanut butter shortage—and threw me one. "Here, eat one. You look like a fucking refugee." She said this every night, and every night I happily obliged.

"That sucks."

"Yeah, well the good news is that he went to jail. That's pretty rare from what I understand." She rummaged through her desk and emerged with a nail file and some purple nail polish. "Do you mind if I paint your nails?"

"That's fine."

"Want to hear the crime report for this week?" she asked as she steadied my big toe. Jeannie was both morbidly fascinated and terrified by all of the crime going on around us; she seemed to find talking about it cathartic. Not waiting for my answer, she launched right in. "Zach's Ecuadorian friend Sergio was robbed at gunpoint in Parque Carolina. They stole his ATM card and made him give them the PIN number and then took the shirt off his back and even his shoes. He didn't even have twenty-five cents for the bus when it was all over, so he had to walk five miles home, barefoot and shirtless. And he's a bodybuilder." The subtext, of course, was that we were not bodybuilders and therefore that much more vulnerable. "The Center's librarian was robbed at knifepoint in the Center's library during her prep period."

"How did he get past the guards?"

She shrugged. "I don't know. And did you hear what happened to Kyle and Katherine last night?" Kyle and Katherine were two of the volunteers. Kyle was a short dark-haired guy from Boston and Katherine was his girlfriend.

"No."

"They were held up at gunpoint in Gringolandia"—'Gringolandia' was our term for the upscale tourist section of Quito's New Town, filled with hotels, bars, and Internet cafés, and supposedly one of the safest areas in Quito—"and then just as Kyle is reaching for his wallet, the guy falls down at their feet. Shot in the back. Apparently the hotel security guard across the street saw what was going on and shot him. On the one hand, he saved them from a robbery. But on the other hand, what if he'd missed?"

Neither of us answered the question.

CHAPTER TWELVE

When I woke up one morning, the world was blurry. The straight lines of the numbers on my alarm clock were wavy and sinuous, and my bookshelves slanted towards me ominously. I held my hand in front of my face. The edges were ill-defined and the skin looked jaundiced.

I bolted out of bed and stumbled to the mirror. There in front of me was a blurry, grainy image, with two swollen holes for eyes, streaked yellow. It was if I were fading into a sepia-toned past, a long-forgotten murkiness, which terrifying as it was, seemed hauntingly appropriate, as if I could no longer function in the clarity of the present and required safer, gentler environs. I reached for a tissue and blotted my eyes. The image became less streaky. Looking down, I saw that the tissue was covered in a strange mucous-like substance.

I dressed and went downstairs to wait for the bus. The others took a step back when they saw me. "What happened?" whispered a horrified Katherine, barely visible through the glaze.

"I don't know. I went to bed and everything was normal. I woke up and....Maybe I'm going blind." Trying to shrug as if it were no big deal, I hopped on the bus and stared straight ahead, resolving to be positive and meditate on the accomplishments of Ray Charles and Helen Keller.

When we arrived, I sprinted up the steps to the nurse's office and banged on the door. There was no answer. "They open at eight," one of the women in the hallway informed me.

Feeling deformed and repulsive, I skulked into the principal's office and hid my face behind a newspaper. I read about a fire that destroyed half of the Parliament building and a small bomb that exploded outside of Jeannie's favorite McDonald's. There are worse things in the world than going blind, I tried to console myself. And it even has some benefits—like not being able to see litter on the side of the road, or watch an Ecuadorian kid wipe his nose on his hand before shaking yours. I was estimating how long it would take me to learn Braille when Lidia walked in. *"Buenos días*, Maureen," she chirped.

"Buenos días," I muttered through the newspaper. We had a whole conversation while I stared as Lucio's pixilated face. She didn't seem to mind talking to a wall of newsprint.

The whistle blew at last and I could hide no more. With my eyes downcast and my hair thrust forward into my face, I trudged to the patio as though condemned. I stood in front of my class, waiting for someone to shriek that a werewolf was in their midst. No one did. In fact, one or two of my students told me my eye was gross, but that was about it. They didn't seem too unnerved by the sight of their teacher struggling to see though a veil of urine-colored sludge, an occasional sickly yellow tear sliding slowly down her face.

At lunchtime, I was finally able to see the nurse. I sat on a rough wooden bench and waited in the hallway. Patricio, one of my ninth-graders, was waiting too. "Why are you here?" I asked.

"Stomach virus."

"Oh." I glanced at him and noticed a scar, about an inch long, next to the cross-shaped tattoo on his cheek. "Where'd you get that?"

He reached up to massage the area. "A bullet grazed me when I was twelve years old. I was at the market buying groceries when all of the sudden a firefight broke up between two rival gang members and I was caught in the middle." He shrugged. "It happens, you know."

I smiled weakly, trying to maintain an expression of sympathy and understanding, all the while knowing I most certainly did not know what it was like to be grazed by a bullet or caught in the middle of a gun battle, and I certainly didn't understand what would possess someone to endanger innocent children like that.

The nurse called my name, led me inside, and gestured for me to have a seat. "So, what can I do for you today?"

I stared at her, uncomprehending. Wasn't it obvious? "Well, I have this pus in my eye..."

She shined a light in my eye, examined it for a second, and said, very confidently, "You have an eye infection common in pigs."

"*Cerdos, chanchos?*" I repeated, dumbfounded, and then just to make sure, added, "The animals that pork comes from?"

"Of course," she said, slightly annoyed, as if to say, where else would you get pork from? "Some of our families sleep with their pigs and get infections from them as a consequence, and one of these students probably gave it to you."

"Am I going blind?"

She laughed. "No. It will only last a few days. I'll give you some drops." She handed me a bottle and I was on my way.

In retrospect, the pus seemed like some kind of omen, a turning point after which everything went south. First it was a trickle of minor thefts: my raincoat went missing, my favorite William and Mary sweatshirt was pilfered, and my favorite blue sweater set was snatched from the laundry room during the chaos of Palm Sunday celebrations, when the laundry became the distribution point for thousands of palm fronds. "Such a shame," Wilson's mother clucked as she folded a pair of plaid boxer shorts. "Everyone knew that the sweater belonged to a volunteer—you're the only ones who have your clothes cleaned here—and yet they stole it right out from under you. Imagine, they stole it from someone who doesn't even get paid to put up with their children's nonsense!" She shook her head again and slammed a dryer shut for good measure.

Then the slow and steady decimation of my *nivelación* class began. It had already been shrinking, with Oscar dying, another student's family being kicked out of the Center, and a third demoted to sixth grade. But now all of this intensified, and in a most unsettling way.

For the third day in a row, I found myself looking at two empty seats, where Raymond and Alejandro, without a doubt my most studious and serious boys, usually sat. "Does anyone know if they are sick or something?" I asked. Everyone shrugged. After a week or two more of this, Jefferson interrupted me during roll call one day. "I heard that they moved." No one looked concerned or sad. There wasn't a whole lot of loyalty amongst this class.

That night, I casually asked Madre Kathy if she knew anything about the whereabouts of Raymond and Alejandro. "Oh, yeah, some of our people told me they moved and they won't be going to the Center anymore. The family didn't speak to me, and they didn't leave a note. No warning, nothing—just up and gone in the middle of the night." She shrugged and went back to her dinner.

And that was just the way it was. No one thought to inform me that two of my students were gone for good, least of all the students themselves. I did not rate a good-bye or an explanation, or even a simple acknowledgement that our paths in life had crossed, had meant something, had enriched each other, and that we would go our separate ways and do just fine. People were expendable and interchangeable; relationships were ephemeral and fleeting. No one was worth remembering, and no one felt worthy of being remembered. I wanted to know that they would enroll in another school and live in a place at least as nice as where they had been, and everyone else just wanted to know why I would want to know such a thing. I wanted finality, closure, and peace of mind, with each of the chapters of my life having a beginning and an end, but Ecuadorians could neither fathom nor indulge this need. Their lives were constant repetitions of work and more work, interspersed with births and deaths and marriages and separations, all of which they accepted with equanimity, and peopled with a great and ever-changing cast of minor characters. They watched their lives unfold as if they were spectators at a dull play who had been given the script ahead of time: no surprises, no plot twists.

A few days later, Eduardo, one of the triplets, showed up early for class. Morose, his black eyes brooding beneath his thick black bangs, he kicked the wall a few times. "Madre Kathy is kicking me out of class," he sulked. "She says I need to work for a year and see if I really want to study." I wasn't that surprised. He had been nearly impossible to teach, and his grades were terrible, partly because he only handed in perhaps every fifth assignment. Half of the time, he wouldn't even do the worksheets that I gave them time to do in class, but would instead sit staring at the ceiling or put his head down on his desk. I started to say something encouraging but he stopped me. "Whatever. I'll see you around." He shuffled out of the room.

Juan and Edison were the ones who broke my heart the most. Like Raymond and Alejandro, Juan disappeared without a word of good-bye, without so much as one last bone-crushing handshake or smarmy comment about Paul. He just went to class less and less until one day he stopped coming at all. I wondered if his girlfriend was pregnant. If she wasn't, it was probably only a matter of time.

Edison was the only one who gave me a proper good-bye. He came into my classroom a few minutes early, as he often did, but this time he didn't ask about Michael Jordan or tell me about Liga's record. He just stared at me in stony silence, his legs dangling over the side of the desk and swinging violently back and forth. He had evidently grown a few inches, because for the first time I noticed that his feet could touch the floor.

"*Estás bien*, Edison?" I asked gently.

He shook his head and I could tell he was trying not to cry. "The Madres are kicking me out."

Part of me was not surprised. Edison had some serious anger issues and he hadn't turned in an assignment all year. Paul's view that he was psychotic seemed to be shared by Don Rodrigo and probably most of the teachers as well. But I had glimpsed another side of Edison. I knew that he was a great big brother, and I sensed that deep down he was just a frightened teenage boy. I wasn't ready to give up on him, and I was angry that everyone else was.

But there was nothing I could do. Once the Madres made a decision, it was made, and they tolerated no dissent. "Good luck," was all I could say to him. "I'll miss you."

Edison gave me a couple of bear hugs and said he'd miss me, and then he slipped out before the other kids saw him. Class went more smoothly without him, but all the same, the empty chair bothered me.

Demoralized from the loss of my students, the persistent threat of violence further dampened my spirits. Four American women we knew were raped, and one volunteer was threatened with a weapon on three separate occasions. I felt like a pawn in a game designed by misanthropes, drawn ever deeper into a plague of paranoia, never sure what was worse: the random violence that seemed to flare up around us, or the loss of freedom, trust, and spontaneity that resulted. I took only taxis at night, but never alone; I shielded my chest with my backpack on the bus, to avoid being groped; I used the store windows to monitor who was behind me. I didn't talk to strangers on the bus, or take walks in the evenings, or go home early from a night out, alone. I had ceased to be the confident, trusting, invincible young woman I had been.

Nonetheless, I was still shocked when I went to confer with Susana about a particularly vexing Spanish grammar question and, upon finding her desk empty, was informed that she was recovering from being gassed.

"Oh, that's common here," Carlos, a handsome and avuncular forty-something teacher who occupied the desk next to hers, said matter-of-factly, as if he were explaining how Ecuadorians celebrate Christmas or mark an anniversary. "They gas you in your sleep so that you won't wake up for a long time. Sometimes they fill the house with too much gas"—he used his rough, tanned hands to simulate the formation of gas clouds, stretching them apart to indicate the growth of the gas cloud, then leaned towards me, lowering his voice—"and the victims never wake up."

"How awful," I said.

Carlos shrugged and went on. "Anyway, apparently she and the other women preparing for the convent woke up and everything was gone. The stove and the refrigerator had been ripped from the wall, the counters were uprooted from the floor, their clothes were gone. Everything, absolutely everything. They just woke up in their beds, islands in the middle of nothing. And you want to know the worst part?" He laughed bitterly and slapped his hand against the desk. "The police published their names and addresses in the paper so now the bastards know they snitched."

"It's seems like the police are setting them up for retribution."

"Probably," he said. "It might even have been off-duty police who gassed them in the first place. That happens, you know. The police have the perfect racket: either they get paid off by the criminals to look the other way, or they commit the crime themselves and make off with the loot, knowing full well their fellow policemen aren't going to turn them in. One way or another, they profit."

At that moment I hated Ecuador. With a fury that had been building for months, I absolutely loathed it, fully and completely. It wasn't that particular crime. Horrific as it was, worse things had happened. It was the culmination of it all: the lecherous old men and the thieving policemen and the conniving politicians and the egregious domestic violence and doctors who let Oscar die in the waiting room and the sense that you were not safe anywhere, at any time, with anyone. I wanted to turn the clock back and pretend I had never been here, pretend I still believed wholeheartedly in the essential goodness of human beings and the possibility of redemption, pretend that justice would prevail and the wicked would get their comeuppance. I wanted to purge the whole experience from memory, vomit forth every morsel of Ecuadorian food I had ever eaten, exhale every bit of Andean air from my lungs, scrub every granule of Ecuadorian soil out of my pores, and erase every bit of evidence of my presence here if that meant that I would once more feel pure and uncontaminated, blissfully naïve and uncorrupted. I wanted to click my heels three times and be magically transported home.

I walked across the playground, a jumble of metal slides and ladders and swings usually swarming with dirt-streaked children in mismatched clothes. Now, enveloped in the sudden stillness of dusk, it sat listless and empty. A lone brown leaf scraped against the pavement and brushed against my leg as I listened to the dull clanging of a rusted swing battered about by the cold wind. It had a mesmerizing quality that drew me towards it. I squeezed myself onto the seat and pushed myself off the ground. Each time my foot hit the sandy dirt, I pushed off harder than the time before, as if I were convinced that if I swung high enough I could propel myself over the walls of the Center, beyond the pink-crested mountains, and over an entire continent of misery and corruption.

The bus from the downtown center arrived and everyone except Jeannie filed inside. She came over and sat on the swing beside me. I told her about Susana as we squinted into the sunset and traced designs in the dirt with our feet. "That sucks," she said softly. We sat in silence for a moment, rocking back and forth.

"If you were Ecuadorian, would you stuff yourself in a gas tank to come to America?" I asked suddenly.

"Yes," she said without hesitating. Jeannie seemed to understand exactly what I meant. "Do you ever get on a bus and think, how many of these men would rape me if given a chance?"

"Yeah."

"So do I. And it scares me to death. It scares me to live in a country where it sometimes seems that hardly anyone gives a fuck about what happens to anyone else."

That seemed to be the definitive statement on everything, so we stopped talking and just swung.

CHAPTER THIRTEEN

My visa was about to expire. Unlike everyone else, who had received the customary two-year "missionary" visa from the consulate in Chicago, I had made the mistake of going to the consulate in Washington, D.C., where I was living at the time. The woman I had dealt with was most unpleasant. A small woman with hard features, she looked right through me and repeated "it's for one year only" in the same monotone voice no matter how many proofs of eligibility for a two-year visa I produced. In the end, I had had no choice but to assent.

When I took my passport to Madre Josefina and showed her the expiration date on my visa, stamped in red ink and looming less than six weeks away, she registered no surprise. "I am sure they were expecting you to offer a bribe," she said dryly. "And of course, it's ridiculous that they are charging volunteers extra, but that's the way it is."

"What do you recommend I do?"

"Pay two hundred dollars and apply for a new visa."

"And if I refuse to do that?"

"See if Don Rodrigo will take you to Colombia on the next trip he makes to visit his in-laws. It's only a two hour drive. Then you spend twenty-four hours there, and cross the border back again with a three-month tourist visa."

"Isn't the border with Colombia rather...unsafe?" I had been reading articles in the paper about how Ecuadorian border towns had become safe havens for the Colombian rebel army the FARC. Many of these towns had FARC-affiliated brothels, restaurants, and hotels all frequented by FARC guerillas sent there for "rest and relaxation," even surgery. It was little comfort to me that they were supposed to be resting from the front; old habits die hard, and for a disciplined group of thugs—the world's leading kidnapping organization—a lone American lounging in a tough border town might prove to be a bit too much of a temptation. And that was just what awaited me on the Ecuadorian side of the border. I didn't even want to think about the Colombian side.

"I suppose." She paused. "Well, you could always try the hard way. Go the Ministry of Foreign Relations and explain that you received a one-year visa in error and require an extension."

The next afternoon I took the bus downtown to a cheery hot-pink colonial building. Two young guards, both clad in bulletproof vests, their machine guns slung casually over their arms, chatted outside. One approached me, smiling broadly. He looked good-natured, a bit flirtatious and not the least bit menacing. "How can I help you, *señorita*? What is your business at the Ministry?"

"I'm trying to get my visa renewed."

He raised an eyebrow and then laughed, a little too long and loud for my comfort. "That is quite a mission now, isn't it? Ask inside at the front desk. They'll tell you whom to speak with."

The inside was far less impressive than the outside. The floor was bare tile and rather worn, and the walls were a nondescript color. The initial reception area resembled a bus station. I waited in line for a few minutes, approached the humorless, mustachioed official at the counter and, after a brief argument, was told to see Señor Garcia upstairs.

I bounded up the steps to the second floor, an unexpectedly homey domain with shag carpeting and furniture from the seventies. Swarthy bureaucrats took long drags on their cigarettes as they thumbed through mounds of paperwork. Accosted by a chubby middle-aged woman who demanded to know what I was doing there, I deftly sidestepped her, yelled something about having an appointment with Señor Garcia, and slid into his office. He stood up abruptly and brushed ashes off his tie in an officious manner. "Who sent you up here?" he demanded.

"Señor Menéndez, downstairs. He said you were the only one who could arrange this."

He frowned, cleared his throat, and sat down. Rather tall for an Ecuadorian, he sported a beer belly, shaggy black eyebrows that wiggled up and down like fat caterpillars above his thick-rimmed glasses, and a thick shock of black hair to match. "Well, then," he said, pushing his papers around, trying to impress on me that he was a very busy and important man, "what can I do for you?"

"It's about my visa, Señor." I pulled out my passport and a letter from the Padre. "As stated here in this letter from Padre José of the _____ Center—you are familiar with the Center, right?"

He nodded uneasily.

"I am a volunteer teacher there, and as a volunteer I am entitled to a two-year visa. When I applied at the consulate, however, they made a mistake and only issued a one-year visa. However, as you know, the school year lasts until July. Therefore, I require a three-month extension."

He regarded me with a supercilious air. "Well, you should have asked for a two-year visa at the consulate."

"I did."

"Well you should have resolved it there," he retorted, annoyed. "It is not my problem that the consulate made a mistake!"

"I understand that it is not your problem. But I understand that you are a very important official here and could assist in resolving the problem." I fixed my best come-hither smile on him, and forced myself to stare dreamily at his revolting bloated face for a full thirty seconds. Your kids need you, I told myself to justify this shameless ploy. Even a nun would try flirting in this situation.

Unfortunately, Señor Garcia was a disgrace to red-blooded Latin males everywhere. He had not the slightest interest in the attention or flattery of a *gringa* half his age, a fact which I regarded as not only unlucky but downright unnatural. In a country in which every corner store and every bus featured pictures of pale-skinned bare-breasted blondes, with some photo collages of these buxom white women verging on veritable shrines, it seemed almost unpatriotic of him to be so blasé about the presence of an exotic American woman in his office. I wondered if these immigration officials were given special training to inure themselves to the charms of nubile young foreigners—perhaps they spent days trapped in a room full of naked blondes and were zapped with electricity every time they reached out to touch one. Alternatively, maybe asexuality was part of the selection criteria, or the Ecuadorian government operated a secret laboratory tucked away in some remote valley where they genetically engineered the next generation of hormone-deficient, colorless officials.

I batted my eyelashes one more time, to no avail, and then moved on to a new tactic. "Señor Garcia, I know you are a compassionate man. I know you understand how important receiving an education is to these children. Education is the only way out of their squalid lives, the only way Ecuador will achieve prosperity and growth." I paused for dramatic effect. "You cannot imagine how difficult their lives are…" I rambled on for a minute or two, painting a picture, with the most pathos I could muster, of misery, ignorance, and poverty, alleviated by the shining presence of an American volunteer dedicating herself selflessly to the betterment of Ecuador's poor. He yawned and I cut short my appeal, concluding with one final "…and this is why I need a three month extension."

Señor Garcia was unmoved, however. In a firm, flat voice, with resolute finality, he said, "There is nothing I can do. The only office that can perhaps help you is the one on Amazonas. Just ask a cab driver. They all know where the Ministry is." He waved me impatiently out of his office.

This second office was a gray concrete hulk of a building on the outside, but inside it looked like an American DMV office. It was pleasant and modern, although somewhat institutional in feel, and they had each of us take a number and wait to be called. When a young army recruit called my number an hour later, I approached the desk, unfolding once again the letter and presenting my passport and visa. He shook his head sympathetically. "I'm sorry, despite what they told you downtown, that was the correct office. Perhaps you spoke to the wrong person. You need to go back and try again."

I walked outside and hailed another cab, pulling up once again in front of the same guards. They laughed hysterically. "Weren't you just here?"

I rolled my eyes and entered the reception area for the second time that day. After waiting for half an hour, I spoke to yet another official who assured me that Señor Garcia was not the right man, and the office on Amazonas was not the right office, but the office on Avenida de las Americas was definitely the correct place to go.

I walked a mile to the Americas office. It was another gray concrete boxy building, completely characterless on the outside, and unlike the Amazonas office, complete characterless on the inside as well. The lighting gave everything a ghastly greenish-gray hue and the plain walls and floors and bare work stations had a decidedly Soviet feel. There was a lone typewriter—manual, not electric—here or there, but no computers to be seen. I wound my way through endless corridors, all mind-numbingly identical, lined with bare, windowless offices, each indistinguishable from the next. At last I emerged at the supposedly correct office and was forced to stand in yet another queue. When I at last reached the front of the line, my passport and letter now sticking to my sweaty palms, I was told by yet another self-important paper-pusher that I was in the wrong line and would have to go to the back of another line.

Gritting my teeth, I made my way slowly to the end of this fifth line of the day and seethed. Just what country did they think they were in anyway?, I silently raged. No one stands in lines here. The only people who want to move here are Colombians fleeing a civil war. I don't want to move here. I don't want to tax their nonexistent social safety net or mug their impoverished citizens. I only want to stay three more months and finish what I started. I only want to teach their children, a job that they don't want to do, and I perform this service free. And they can hardly plead overcrowding. It seemed like half of the population was already in Italy or Spain or the U.S., and the other half was making plans to be there soon, and that this exodus made plenty of room for a few foreigners like me.

Something inside me snapped. "Just give me the damn visa already!" I heard myself yell, and I had the strange sensation of feeling far, far away, disconnected from myself, as if I were a sane person calmly contemplating a lunatic having a meltdown in a government office. The woman ahead of me in line turned and nodded sympathetically. "Everyone is trying to leave this country—everyone, absolutely everyone—and I am the only person trying to stay!" I shouted.

I felt triumphant for a moment as my words echoed lightly through the room and a few of the other oppressed line-dwellers murmured their assent, no doubt thinking of their own elaborate plans to flee the country.

The bureaucrats, however, saw neither my beaming face not the glimmer of sympathy in the eyes of my companions. They didn't even look up from their desks.

CHAPTER FOURTEEN

I met Hot William in the boys' bathroom. He, of course, introduced himself as William, just William, for he did not know that he had acquired the moniker Hot William. The "hot" had been part of his name since the first week of our arrival, when one of the female volunteers had been going on and on about a guy named William and I had stupidly asked, "Which one?" Every female within earshot had answered in unison, "the hot one" and one of his great admirers added that I would know which one he was when I spotted him.

Oddly enough, I did know when I saw him. He was perched precariously on a ledge overlooking a stairwell near the front gate, his head propped up on one elbow and the rest of his athletic body stretched out like a lizard sunbathing on a rock. Engrossed in an English book, he absentmindedly pushed a stray lock of hair out of his liquid brown eyes as the late afternoon sun gave his dark brown hair a golden glow. His skin was perfectly bronzed, and he looked up to flash a smile at me. It was a dazzling smile, the kind you never see in real life, only in toothpaste commercials or in movies, and even then you know that such a smile was only obtained after years of braces and teeth whitening treatments. But Hot William's was the real deal: he had been blessed by God and nature with a set of teeth able to withstand years of unfluoridated water, poor nutrition, and a complete lack of dental care, and here he was flashing that smile, so blindingly white against his mahogany skin, so ostentatious compared to the cavity-ridden, yellow teeth of the other students or the gaping holes of their parents.

It was strange, really. He didn't even know my name, and yet I knew quite a bit about him. From the frequent gossipy conversations the female volunteers had about Hot William, I learned that he was twenty-one, in ninth-grade (but not in my class, I had the two younger ninth-grade sections and another teacher taught the third—oldest—section), studying to be a carpenter, and very interested in learning English. I also knew that he was from a large family and that his mother, who couldn't have been more than sixty but appeared absolutely ancient, suffered from a sort of dementia, which everyone except the volunteers seemed to fail to notice, or perhaps had noticed long ago but had since ceased to find anything interesting in her odd behavior. That was the way it was with the Center members, and it was refreshing in a way. Physical and mental impairments were accepted as part of a person's identity, something that they had never thought of as curable or treatable or even diagnosable. Rather than insisting, as Americans do, that every misfortune in life could be prevented or fixed or at the very least labeled so that everyone would know and understand and be able to fit so-and-so with the gimpy leg or the forgetful memory into a rational, definable category, almost a new species or genus, Ecuadorians preferred to accept people as they were; they didn't know they had a choice. They would refer to each other as "the blond one" or "the fat one" or "the guy with the gimpy leg" or "the crazy woman." Nobody suffered from obesity or cerebral palsy or psychosis. They just lived with their own peculiarities, and they died with them, and if you asked someone what their loved one died from, it was a rather strange question indeed. Most people just died. They were sick beforehand, to be sure, but it did not matter much with what, because regardless of the illness, whether hepatitis or bronchitis or plain old diarrhea, death came pretty much the same, and if it didn't, the illness through which one had passed was soon forgotten in the daily grind of survival.

And so it was that now, many months after this brief initial encounter, we once again crossed paths, and this time in the least glamorous of settings. I was standing over Jefferson, inspecting his cleaning job on the urinal when Hot William brushed past me on the way to a shower stall. "*Hola!*" he greeted me, surprised to see a volunteer in such a setting early on a Saturday morning, and flashed his hundred-watt smile in my direction, extending his hand. "*Yo soy William,*" he said with great self-confidence.

I wanted to say, of course you're William, I know that, and are you aware that all of the volunteers, even the guys, refer to you as Hot William? But I didn't. Instead I stepped gingerly over a rust-colored pool of filth and shook his hand firmly, professionally almost, as though we were meeting at a networking event rather than in a fetid lavatory. "*Y yo soy la voluntaria Maureen.*"

"Maureen, Maureen," he repeated joyously, with the same enraptured smile on his face. "What a beautiful name! And you have such beautiful eyes! Do you have a boyfriend?"

Raúl and Jefferson exchanged gleeful glances as they scrubbed the floor behind Hot William.

"No."

"No? I cannot believe that! What do you think of Ecuadorian men? Do you want an Ecuadorian boyfriend?"

This was my cue to launch into my frequently-delivered speech about how few Ecuadorian men were loyal, how so many beat their wives, and how different the balance of power between the sexes was here than in America. I usually gave this speech for two reasons: first, it tended to dampen the amorous hopes of a would-be lothario, and second, there was always a slight possibility, or so I thought, to make the object of this lecture rethink his views of women.

With Hot William, however, the conversation took a decidedly different turn. Rather than listening with eyes glazed over, or nodding along unenthusiastically in an attempt to placate me, Hot William was delighted to listen to my harangue and consider its merits. From time to time he asked me questions to clarify my position. "So you are saying you wouldn't mind if your husband stayed at home?" he inquired, puzzled, as I delved into my house husband fantasy. "You'd rather he watch the children while you work?" I nodded and he laughed. "Wow!" he marveled, using his favorite American word. "Well, why not? I guess that's only fair. Why are women always expected to be the one to stay home?" He pondered this for a moment and then pronounced me a very smart woman.

And thus began an unexpected friendship between Hot William and me. It befuddled the *nivelación* boys, who were now conflicted as to whether they should continue teasing me about "Pablo" or move on to tormenting me about William. They settled, naturally, on inventing a big scandal whereby I had left Pablo for William and poor Pablo was absolutely heart-broken. Paul thought it was very funny. "What's this I hear, Maureen? You left me for Hot William and I had to find out through the kids?" he joked one night at dinner before dissolving into laughter.

The more I got to know Hot William, the less I thought of him as a pretty face and the more I thought of him as an extraordinary—and very out-of-place—individual. He was by far the strangest Ecuadorian I met all year. He exclaimed rather than spoke; every sentence was punctuated by a question mark or an exclamation point and peppered full of "wow's". He looked authority figures straight in the eye, as if defying them to see him as their equal, rather than looking down like everybody else. He walked purposefully, with a spring in his step, rather than dragging his feet. He was curious about absolutely everything, wanted to know the English word for absolutely everything, and unlike virtually every single Ecuadorian I knew, read books.

But by far the most notable thing about Hot William was that he was high on life, on the combustible mix of hope and possibility and ambition, and full of confidence. I was always amazed at how easily he talked about all of the past tragedies of his life and how elated he could be at all times, regardless of the circumstances. One night, as we walked past the shuttered shops on Avenida de la Prensa, I asked him about his family and how they came to the Center. "I'm one of eight," he told me. "My mom had four other children, but they died. One of them was only a few weeks old. One day, she started coughing, and a few days later she died while I was holding her."

"Did your mom take her to a doctor?"

"No."

"What about your dad?"

"He died when I was nine. I left school and went to work to support my mom and a few other siblings. Then when I was sixteen, my mom discovered the Center, and I was able to work and go to school too." He laughed. "That's why I am twenty-one and in the ninth grade."

At times like these Hot William would wax poetic about the Center and all the opportunities it had given him. He saved his most animated expression, however, for the times that he discussed his future grandiose employment plans. Each time we passed a furniture shop, he would be reminded of his great plan. "Did I tell you about my plan?" he would say. "I am going to apprentice myself to a carpenter for a few years, learn about the business, then start renting his equipment after hours to create my own hand-crafted pieces. I'll slowly build a client base, start saving up money, and eventually have enough to open my open business. One day I am going to have a store just like this. No, wait, one day I will have ten stores just like this!"

At the end of these long conversations, it was hard to believe that Hot William went home to the same shantytown as the rest of my students. Yet I knew that he lived in the same type of rudimentary hovel, he leapt over the same open sewers, he rode the same creaky buses, he drank the same contaminated water, and he wore the same mismatched ragged hand-me-downs from middle-class Milwaukeeans who couldn't even locate Ecuador on a map. He and they were alike in circumstance, but so different in outlook. He and I were alike in outlook, but so different in circumstance.

Sometimes the difference in circumstances came into painfully sharp relief. While sitting on the sidelines of a soccer game one day, he matter-of-factly told me that most of his childhood friends were now drug dealers. "I thought about it too, you know," he said. "Who wouldn't? They make a lot of money; they see it as a business. But then I joined the Center and began studying to be a carpenter. It's a good thing too. Most of them are dead or in jail now. It's strange how that all goes down. The cops are too afraid to go into our neighborhood, so they hover over the house of the drug dealer with a helicopter. When they caught my friend José Luis, it felt like a war zone. They must have ended up sending thirty policemen in."

"How do the neighbors react when they find out a drug dealer or a thief is living next to them?" I asked.

"Usually people don't bother with the drug dealers. Sometimes though..." his voice trailed off. "One time a kid—maybe twelve or fourteen years old—stole some of the coins that the residents had placed in a neighborhood shrine to the Virgin Mary as an offering. Everyone was outraged, and a mob gathered around him. Someone poured gasoline on him, and then they lit him on fire."

"Did anyone try to intervene?" I stammered, aghast.

"No."

"Was anyone arrested?"

"No," he said as if that were a foregone conclusion. "Someone actually videotaped the scene, but more than eighty people participated in the attack, so it was hard to assign blame. Of course, they could have just arrested all eighty, but the police didn't want to anger the whole neighborhood and spark retaliation, so no one was ever punished." He shrugged and laughed his big laugh and smiled his big smile. "Wow! Crazy, huh?"

Crazy, indeed.

As unique as Hot William's lofty career goals were, I soon discovered that his childhood career dilemma—to be a criminal, or not to be—was anything but.

The day I had this epiphany began uneventfully enough, with Lidia lining up the elementary school girls in the courtyard, pairing them off, and instructing each girl to look after her partner. We were about to embark on a "fieldtrip"—otherwise known as a long, sweaty hike—to the top of the Panecillo, an earthen knob just south of the city center with a panoramic view of the colonial quarter. Some of the older girls whined and moaned as their partner for the day was announced, but most took the news in stride and solemnly took the little girl's mucous-stained hand in her own. I felt rather solemn myself, remembering the cheery disclaimer in my travel guide urging tourists to take a taxi to this "highly-recommended" site in order to bypass "the rabid dogs and armed individuals" that roamed the path to the top. When I added to this Lidia's comment the day before about perverts assaulting little girls in the same general vicinity, my stress level increased further. "Are you sure we should be doing this?" I asked Lidia. "Why don't we just walk them a couple of blocks to the cathedral? It's close and heavily-policed, and they could get some culture along with their exercise."

Lidia regarded me with her usual bemused expression. "Don't be so paranoid, Maureen. They'll be sixty of us bounding up the path."

When she put it like that, it did seem a bit silly. And even if it didn't, I really didn't have a choice in the matter.

So there we went, marching through Old Town like a ragtag midget army, swinging arms and stomping feet, halting traffic at every turn. Old toothless men emerged from the dank interiors of their corner stores to admire the parade, and stern grandmothers in housedresses perched on the balconies above and peered at the spectacle. Oblivious to it all, we sang call-and-response marching ditties at the top of our lungs.

Señor Comandante
　　Señor Comandante
Vamos a la guerra
　　Vamos a la guerra
Cargando papayas
　　Cargando papayas
Para la merienda
　　Para la merienda
O-o-ay-ay
　　O-o-ay-ay
O-o-ah-ah
　　O-o-ah-ah
Que lo repita—
　　Que lo repita—

At this point in the song, the girls would designate a new song leader. They soon learned to choose volunteers, since by this point in the year we had dispensed with all pretensions to human dignity and could no longer be embarrassed by anything, not even screaming at the top of one's lungs in downtown Quito like a madman. The few girls chosen to lead the group just laughed and covered their faces and nudged a volunteer to take on the responsibility for them.

After a very long, hot hike, we finally made it to the top of the Panecillo. I was relieved; we hadn't been mugged and no one had been bitten by a rabid dog. In my opinion, that constituted success.

I walked around the top with a few girls, trying to pick out their houses down below. The city stretched before us: ahead of us, the spires of whitewashed four hundred-year old churches punctuated a skyline of sloping red-tiled roofs neatly lining a grid of narrow streets. Behind us, the homes were equally colorful, but flat, concrete roofs predominated, the rational grid of the Spanish gave way to haphazard hilly lanes, and rubbish pockmarked the landscape. Bulbous cisterns squatted on the buildings in the more modern quarter, and laundry fluttered across rooftops. "That's my house!" one of the girls said excitedly. Then she frowned and pointed at another blue house high up on the hill with a few animals grazing in the yard. "No, that's my house!"

"No. That's *my* house!" her friend insisted. They all looked pretty much the same.

We wandered some more, and I tried to keep the peace each time a fight broke out as to whose house we were looking at. I yelled at them for climbing on some sort of scaffolding. I stood guard while several girls peed against a wall. Volunteering is rarely glamorous.

Then it was time to go. We put the girls in pairs once again and marched them resolutely down the hill, coaxing the most exhausted girls along.

As we approached the Plaza de Santo Domingo, we walked down a street lined with at least forty loitering women. Clad in knee-high boots, fishnet stockings, mini-skirts, and halter tops, they wore heavy make-up; rolls of fat oozed out between the too-too-tight skirts and the too-too-tight tops. Preening, they eyed the male volunteers hopefully. Eleven o'clock in the morning was a bit early for business, and there was a lot of competition. The guys looked a bit green and glued their eyes to the pavement.

An eight-year-old girl tugged at my arm. "How much does a prostitute cost in the States?" she asked.

To my surprise, she said it matter-of-factly, innocently even, not betraying the slightest embarrassment, as if she were asking the price of a stick of gum. She did not appear to doubt for an instant that I would know the answer.

"I don't know," I stammered. "Probably a lot more than here. Maybe twenty dollars an hour."

She looked very impressed, and I hoped I had not just inspired her to be an American prostitute when she "grew up." Maybe Ecuadorian kids didn't ever think of becoming a fireman or an astronaut, but at least they could dream of being beauticians or auto mechanics or some other non-illegal profession. I thought about telling her that there were plenty of jobs that pay twenty dollars an hour that don't involve violent pimps, a high risk of being murdered, sexually transmitted diseases, and unplanned pregnancy, but she had already skipped ahead and was chatting away to some friend of hers, probably describing this wonderful new career path I had just alerted her to.

We returned to the downtown center, and I told the other volunteers to go on home without me. I made some sort of excuse about needing to stay and prepare a lesson plan for my English class, but the truth was that I wanted to take the bus home by myself. Dangerous as they could be, I found Ecuadorian bus rides to be strangely cathartic. There was something about the languid pace as we wound our way through sun-dappled, traffic-clogged streets that transformed it into a meditative, strangely comforting journey through time and space. In an hour, I was transported from the sixteenth century to the twenty-first, from the center of the city to the periphery, from my chaotic morning of estrogen-fueled interpersonal drama to an afternoon filled with lesson planning and testosterone-fueled chaos. It was the only time all day I could really hear myself think.

And so when the other volunteers were all gone, I hopped on a bus and sat by myself, ruminating on the fact that my students did not think about the same things I had thought about at that age. I didn't know what sex was until I was nine and probably didn't know about prostitution until I was eleven or twelve. I never would have thought to ask how much it paid.

Looking around at the passengers, I tried to imagine what they were thinking about. My students would probably be just like them someday. I stared at their faces, scrutinizing their opaque expressions and interpreting the hard lines around their eyes and mouth. They were lines of worry, of pain, of resignation, of dignity, of quiet wisdom and yes, even of laughter. It was likely that few had beyond a sixth-grade education. Judging by my experience with Ecuadorians, they probably had little access to reading material and little interest in reading anyway. So they did not think about books, or the faraway lands and foreign lives described in books and magazines, or the current events detailed in newspapers. They did not think about their weekend plans, for they never had any. Going out requires money, and they didn't have any. They probably did not think about their plans for the future, because most Ecuadorians didn't seem to believe in the future.

The illiterate couldn't even look out the window and read the street signs. I, and others like me, lived in a world of words, but their world was one of meaningless symbols bewilderingly strung together. The signs did not tell them what street they are on or when the pharmacy was open or how to get to the zoo (not that they could pay the admission anyway). All the signs told them was that they were ignorant, that they ought to KEEP OUT of this modern world of knowledge, that they ought to YIELD to those who know more than they. It was like knowing there is a big joke that you aren't in on and never will be. I tried to imagine what it would be like to not be able to read, squinting at the street signs to see if I could temporarily blur my vision. It didn't work.

Looking again at the sad old eyes and the cracked skin, the elaborately embroidered blouses and the thick flannel skirts, I realized that I would never really know what they were thinking. Even if I had asked them, they wouldn't have been able to tell me. Startled and frightened looks, and intense confusion, would have been the only responses to such a strange question. No one ever asks them what they think about anything, much less what they think about.

Most likely, I decided, their thoughts revolved around financial worries, their family, their work, and their small circle of friends. Or maybe—just maybe—coming to America.

Stalin typified the rich Ecuadorian to me. Tall and thin, he wore a tailored suit and an expensive wristwatch, and he surveyed the scene with an air of studied boredom as he waited for me—the mystery guest—to arrive. Rather than approaching me, he waited for me to approach him and ask if he was indeed the famous Stalin, an old classmate of my friend Freddy, even though I would have thought that as a *gringa*, I was the more conspicuous of us two.

He made a big show of opening the door for me and ushering me into the French bakery and sandwich shop, stocked with baskets of golden loaves and staffed by efficient, attractive European-looking women in elegant uniforms. A sandwich combo cost four whole dollars, so eating here was considered a status symbol. It didn't matter that it was technically what Americans would consider high-end fast-food, and in fact maybe it helped. Fast food restaurants were almost exclusively the domain of the elite in Quito: McDonald's was luxury.

After he gallantly paid for my sandwich, we took our plastic trays out onto the balcony overlooking the street, a palm tree-lined boulevard in the chicest area of town. The boutiques of the mall—as expensive as anything you would find in the States—glittered behind us, the stadium sat crumbling just up the street, and blocks of high-rise luxury condos loomed across the boulevard.

I searched for something to say to him. "So…do you still live in Freddy's old neighborhood?"

He nodded and nibbled demurely on his sandwich, while I tried to control the gobs of mayonnaise spurting out of my sandwich. "It's just too expensive to live on one's own."

"Oh, are you a student?"

"Oh, no," he said proudly. "I'm a lawyer."

"Don't you earn enough to live on your own?" I was confused. Hadn't I seen some fliers a few days before advertising luxury apartments for just $200 a month?

"Well, after expenses, not really. Besides, why pay for something you don't have to?" He leaned in and looked at me eagerly like a little boy. "Guess how much I make."

"Four hundred a month."

"More."

"More? Okay, um, eight hundred."

"More."

"Two thousand."

"Nope." He grinned and leaned in just a little more. "Three thousand dollars. And I'm just getting started; I'm only twenty-eight. What do you think of that?"

"I think that you if you donate two thousand to the Center each month, you'll still have more than enough to live on." The moment I said it, I realized it was unfair. After all, I hadn't donated two thousand dollars a month to charity before coming to Ecuador. Although there was something deeply unsettling about the proximity of the fabulously wealthy and the indigent in Ecuador, from a purely logical perspective, I had to admit that there was no reason to hold Ecuador's rich to a higher moral standard than the rich elsewhere in the world.

But if Stalin thought my comment was unfair, he didn't show it. He laughed uproariously, then became slightly more serious. "It's really expensive to live in Quito, you know," he said earnestly. I wondered if he really thought I would believe this, but then I wondered if he might even believe it himself. "It's expensive…friends always calling you, wanting to go out, go somewhere for the weekend, you know."

I told Stalin that my monthly budget was $200 per month and that I hadn't lived with my parents in seven years. He laughed so hard he spit a mouthful of his sandwich out. "You've lived on your own for the past seven years?" he repeated incredulously. "You? You're nothing but a little girl. Look at you! You look like you're twelve. How could you possibly take care of yourself? That's ridiculous."

I felt myself turning red. "It is most certainly true. And if I were you, I would get out of your parents' house and try being independent. It might do you some good."

It was a little harsh, and I knew it, but I also suspected he wouldn't even really understand what I was saying, and I was right. He just laughed again, no doubt thinking I was a silly girl, and dunked his French fries in mayonnaise.

After an hour of suffering through his attempts to impress me, I made a pathetic excuse about needing to dash off to the ATM on the way back to school. He insisted on driving me in his car, which allowed him to launch into a rant about his horrible car that broke down yet again on the dirt roads to his vacation home in Santo Domingo and that he really must replace with a luxury model sometime soon. I consoled him that he was one of the only Ecuadorians I knew that even had a car, and certainly the only one I knew with a vacation home to drive to.

"You'll come see me at my office, right?" he asked as I leapt onto the curb, eager to give him the slip at last. "So I can introduce you to my coworkers?"

"I'll think about it," I lied, knowing that there was no way I could be coaxed into making an appearance as his trophy American girlfriend.

Sadly, most rich Ecuadorians I met reminded me of Stalin. Most had heard of the Center and thought it was fabulous that we were volunteering there. Had they ever thought to volunteer there? No. Had they ever donated? No. My favorite oft-repeated comment was, "Isn't it funny how all of these foreigners come from thousands of miles away to volunteer? We live right here in Quito and haven't ever considered it."

There were others, of course, who inhabited Stalin's world, but took very different lessons from it. The head Center doctor, Giuiliana, could have made an excellent salary in private practice but instead spent most of her time working for a few hundred dollars a month at the Center. The woman who did most of the Center's Ecuador-based fundraising was from a very wealthy family but volunteered her time. And then there was Ana María, a Catholic University medical student who wanted to practice medicine in underserved areas; she and I practiced our language skills on one another. She found my stories about my students disturbing and strangely eye-opening; she knew about as much about their lives as the average person living in Cleveland. One day, she recounted that she had witnessed an event that had made her think of me: a man had brought his daughter, the man who had raped his daughter, and several witnesses to the police station, but the police had refused to so much as question the man and paid no attention to the distraught fellow until a mob descended on the suspect and began to beat him with umbrellas. Then the police had finally taken the man into custody, more for his own protection than any other reason. It was a sad commentary that this episode was inextricably linked in her mind to my life at the Center.

But regardless of whether they adopt the cavalier attitude towards the poor espoused by Stalin or the concerned attitude of Ana María, the inescapable fact is that rich Ecuadorians have very little in common with poor Ecuadorians—ninety percent of the population—save a tense existence on a violent piece of earth. Unlike the rich, these people do not loll about in their vacation homes, or whine about their vehicles, or find umbrella-wielding mobs out of the ordinary. They just dream about being anywhere but Ecuador—anywhere, in fact, where Ecuadorians aren't.

There was one thing that rich and poor had in common, however: an all-purpose refrain to explain away all calamities in the sphere of public life: "This country is a piece of shit." No one ever said "my country" and they definitely never said "our country." "Our" was a virtually unknown pronoun. As the Ecuadorian journalist and philosopher Jorge Enrique Adoum once wrote, "our" is an alien concept to his compatriots, one that implies ownership and with that ownership, responsibility. "Our" also implies collective ownership, that there is only one country and that it is shared by all Ecuadorians.

And that is the problem. There is one Ecuador in the Afro-Ecuadorian shantytown of Don Lino and Juan and the woman in the muumuu, and quite another in the garbage-strewn indigenous shantytowns springing up on the mountainsides, and yet another proudly proclaiming itself in the glitzy malls and hoity-toity clubs of the center. There are Shuar tribes in the east that muddle along indifferent to the government and its edicts, except when yet another oil company is given permission to poison its rivers. There are tribes in the mountains that stone people (non-fatally) for stealing. There are dangerous drug-smuggling ports on the coast that respect no laws or national borders. There are banana barons living it up in style in the steamy lowlands to the west, and rugged oil workers following the pipeline in the east, dragging prostitutes and bandits with them as they go. It has been that way ever since the Spanish arrived, and even before: the Otavalans—now the best-known indigenous group in Ecuador, thanks to the commercial success of their handicrafts—were originally a rebellious tribe in Bolivia forcibly resettled by the nervous Incas to a more remote corner of the empire.

There were times when I too was tempted to fall into this habit. It is easy to talk in the passive voice, to skip all pronouns, to resort to blaming an anonymous "they" or to blaming no one at all, just accepting things as they are. Sometimes, when I was forced to admit that my dreams of an uncorrupt, peaceful, just Ecuadorian society were a long way off, I would find the words "this country..." forming on my lips and feel ashamed—ashamed at my pessimism—and also afraid, infused with the sudden knowledge that I had been there a little too long.

CHAPTER FIFTEEN

By the end of spring, the Big House had turned into a veritable hotel. Every week a new busload would arrive, disgorge a phalanx of pimply, gangly students from some Midwestern Jesuit high school or college on our doorstep, and speed off. Then we were inevitably left to stand nervously by as the newcomers traipsed into the kitchen, devoured the leftovers we were planning on eating for lunch, and glued themselves to the couches in the TV room, to be pried off only when prodded by a chaperone. Occasionally a flashpoint of tension turned amusing, such as the time Paul got roaring drunk on a Saturday afternoon and lectured Madre and Padre about how a certain group of volunteers had failed to help with the dishes, but most of the time the tension was suppressed and the lack of lunch food became just one more minor indignity heaped onto the daily routine.

Some of the guests we enjoyed quite a bit, however. We found a group of high school boys from Marquette High School in Milwaukee to be fabulous houseguests and volunteers, courteous and charming and sincerely interested in our work and the lives of the families we served. A retired couple from New York State made for delightful dinner companions, and the husband performed some much-needed maintenance on our washing machines.

And then there was Karen, a Spanish teacher from rural Wisconsin, and her seventeen-year-old son Sean, whom I liked from the first moment we met. Radiating a certain Midwestern wholesomeness and warmth, they were straightforward and unassuming, eager to help but anxious not to be in the way. Sean was tall, athletic, and blond, a perfect all-American farm boy, with a

147

gravity and seriousness about him, while his mother was a stout, cheery woman with a hearty laugh and lots of enthusiasm. She and Sean had signed on to volunteer for two months, and when Madre Josefina had told me that Sean was a math whiz and interested in helping with my *nivelación* class, I jumped at the chance to have double the number of eyes on my crafty charges.

Later that afternoon, I showed him into our classroom and he took a seat, looking around uncertainly. Jefferson scampered into the room. "*Hola*, Maureen!" he squeaked as he flung his backpack onto a desk. He eyed Sean warily and thrust a grease-strained index finger in his direction. "*Who* is that?"

"Sean. He's going to help us with our class."

"How old is he?"

"Seventeen."

Jefferson didn't seem to like that answer. His eyes narrowed as he regarded Sean—whom he now knew was two feet taller than he was but only four years older—intently. "*Gigante*," he finally whispered, half to himself, half to me, as an explanation of the great disparity in stature.

"He understands Spanish, you know. You can ask him questions yourself."

Jefferson just shrugged, sat down, and ignored us both.

Strangely enough, Sean seemed to provoke the same initial outrage, followed by studied indifference, in every single one of the boys. "What is *he* doing here?" Raúl pouted like a jealous lover. "Is he a new student?"

"No, he's a volunteer that's going to help us."

"I don't need any help. Not from him, anyway."

I pursed my lips and motioned for him to take a seat.

"Is he your new boyfriend?" Darwin demanded.

I nearly choked at the suggestion. "No...he's seventeen."

"So?"

"So he's a little young."

"He doesn't look seventeen." Darwin glanced at him out of the corner of his eye, as if waiting for Sean to admit he was lying about his age. "He's too big."

"Well, he's from Wisconsin. They have more protein there."

He screwed up his face, unsure how to respond to this new bit of information since he didn't know what protein was or how or why it had turned Sean into a giant. He stamped his foot impatiently. "So he's not your boyfriend?"

"No."

Raúl perked up. "So you're still with Pablo?"

"No, she's with Hot William," Raúl explained impatiently.

"My sister says she's dating one of the teachers at the downtown center."

"I still think Sean is her boyfriend..."

Ignoring them, I began tracing triangles and rectangles and circles on the board as I patiently instructed the boys to calculate the area and perimeter of each object. I glanced over at Sean, who sat alone in the corner, befuddled by all of the jealousy and rage his mere presence, seemingly innocuous, could stir up, and no doubt wondering how it was that I had such an intriguing love life.

For the next few weeks, poor Sean suffered much of the same. Every day he sat attentively at the back of the room in a desk so small for his lanky frame that it looked like dollhouse furniture. Every day he would try to strike up a friendly conversation with one of the boys about soccer or marbles. The more mature among them might humor him with a brief conversation, but most of them steadfastly insisted on snubbing him, or worse, imitated what they perceived as his overly polite speech or his flat American accent. Every day I would try to take advantage of his presence by having him work through extra problems with a few of the boys who were struggling, or check the answers of my overly excited students, and every day this strategy was met with more failure than success. Some of the boys begrudgingly let him explain a concept to them, but most leaned low over their papers, stretched an arm across the desk to shield the worksheet from his view, and scowled, as if afraid he might copy from them. "Let Sean help you," I cooed every time this happened, in my faux-patient voice. "He's very good at math." But they never seemed to believe me.

On one of these days, I strolled the aisles, checking answers to word problems while Sean sat listlessly in the corner, observing the usual routine: the violent erasing, the head banging, the hand raising, the triumphant shouting. I was quite sure his classroom at home was nowhere near this lively.

I looked over Darwin's shoulder and saw that he had multiplied when he should have added, subtracted when he should have divided. He clearly did not understand the logic behind the problems. He looked up at me hopefully and I shook my head. His face fell. "No, see, when someone buys a bunch of items at different prices, you need to add the prices, but if it is many items at the same price—"

Raúl tugged at my arm. "Maureen, you promised you'd help me ten minutes ago!"

"Maureen! Maureen! Maureen!" Jefferson was intoning over and over again like a broken doorbell.

"Maureen! You promised you'd help me next!" Wilson whined.

I sighed. Technically, it was true that they were all ahead of Darwin in line, although clearly he needed the most help. They just needed assurance that they were doing fine.

Exasperated, I motioned Sean over to Darwin's desk. "Do you think you could sit with Darwin for ten minutes and work through these problems?"

Darwin threw his pencil at me. "No!" he screamed vehemently, stomping his feet on the floor and curling his lips into a pout. "HE CANNOT HELP ME!" He sprang up from his seat and stumbled blindly out of the room, tripping over backpacks as he went.

I knew that Darwin wasn't particularly fond of Sean, but still, this was hardly the reaction I had expected. What had gotten into him?

I told Sean he was in charge and set off sprinting down the corridor. "Darwin! DARWIN!"

He didn't turn around, but just began running faster, his tiny little legs bounding forward like a jack rabbit. I lengthened my stride, flew past an open doorway of gaping students, and with one final lunge, thrust out a hand to grab Darwin by the waist. The full force of his little body collided with my arm and I winced in pain. Furious, he twisted around to face me and for the first time I saw that tears were pouring down his face. His little chest cavity, sheathed in a faded Galápagos Islands T-shirt smudged with automobile grease, was heaving violently. "L-l-let me g-g-go," he stuttered, as he fought for a breath between giant sobs. His little fists pummeled my arms as he tried to wriggle free of my grip. "L-l-let me g-g-g-o!" With this last sob, he collapsed into a giant sobbing heap on the floor and I slid down to sit next to him on the cold linoleum. The wet splotches on his T-shirt grew.

"Darwin, what's wrong?" I shook him slightly, truly worried. Maybe there was something going on at home that I didn't know about. Maybe his mother was dying, or maybe she had a new boyfriend who was using Darwin as a punching bag. "Is everything okay at home?"

He nodded and let loose another wail. He shook violently, and he banged his head against the wall. I put my hand behind his head, afraid he might give himself a concussion.

"Darwin, what's wrong? You can trust me. I want to help. What's bothering you?"

"You—you—you—" he struggled to get the words out, "you don't care about me anymore!"

"That's why you're crying? You think I don't care about you anymore?"

He nodded miserably.

I suppressed a smile, relieved that it was nothing more serious than that. Hugging him tightly, I said earnestly, "Of course, I do."

"No, you don't! You always send Sean! Always! You help everyone else, but not me. When I call your name and say I want you to come here, that means I want YOU to come here. That means I want MY teacher! You--" he pointed an accusatory finger at me, "are MY teacher!" He stamped his foot defiantly, then looked down and angrily wiped away a thick layer of salty tears with the back of his hand.

"Darwin, I—I love you," I said softly, hoping that didn't sound too creepy. He looked up hopefully. "You're my *marido*. You're one of my favorite students. I'm so proud of how hard you've been working. I just thought Sean could help you do better, because it's really important to me that you do well."

He sniffled and looked at me suspiciously.

"I promise from now on, I'll try to pay more attention to you in class. But remember that there are lots of other students who need help."

He gave me half a nod, as if indicating that he understood my position but was only partially mollified and that, if I really wanted to get back in his good graces, it would take a lot more than that.

"Deal?"

"Deal," he muttered begrudgingly. We shook hands.

"*Marido*, let's go back to class." I grasped his grubby arm and steered him back down the hallway, trying to suppress a smile. It was always the tough guys who were the most sensitive, I thought. No matter how many problems they cause you, they expect you to love them unconditionally, and when they think you don't, they throw a hissy fit.

I opened the door and was greeted with a paper airplane flying straight into my face. There were pieces of paper flying everywhere, children clambering on top of desks, kids chasing each other around the room, and desks being shoved every which way. Sean stood in the middle of the mayhem, trying to direct everyone back to their seats. No one seemed to even notice he was there. It was just like the old days.

I slammed the door and everyone sat down. Sean stared in amazement. "I thought they were bad before, but apparently not."

"Oh, no, what you see every day is their best behavior, trust me. Don't feel bad, though: this was exactly what they were like for me at the beginning of the year."

Darwin skulked into a seat in the corner and hunched over his worksheet, periodically wiping the tears from his face with an irritated flick of the wrist. He was disgusted with himself for crying, for showing himself to be so vulnerable and so needy, but there was nothing he could do to stop the waterworks. His classmates peered at his blotchy, purple face from time to time, but respectfully said nothing. Eventually he stopped crying.

Sean took a step towards him at one point. I shook my head, and he moved on.

Later that night, I lay sprawled out on Jeannie's bed recounting Darwin's bizarre outburst in minute detail while she hunkered down on the floor, grading stacks of papers. "He actually started sobbing?" she asked, incredulous. "This was the boy who stole the Atari and made you strip search everyone, right?"

"Well, actually the Inspector—"

"Whatever. He's the thief, right?"

"Right."

She smiled. "Aww, that's so cute." Jeannie scrawled a note across the top of one of the tests in red ink, followed by three exclamation points. Then she stuck a big Daffy Duck sticker at the top. She hopped up, crossed the room to raid her secret stash of

Reese's peanut butter cups and threw me one. "Here, eat one. Pretty soon they are going to put you on one of those Ethiopian famine commercials."

"But I'm not Ethiopian."

"Maybe there will be a famine in Moldova or something. You look vaguely Moldovan."

"I do?"

"Sure," Jeannie said, but I could tell her mind was already on something else. "So...I've made a big decision," she said dramatically as she plopped back down on the floor. She let the gravity of the moment sink in for a moment, although in all honesty, I wasn't expecting too earth-shattering of an announcement. "I've decided to stay another year."

"*What?*"

"I've decided to stay another year."

"But you hate this country. Absolutely hate it."

"Absolutely fucking hate it," Jeannie corrected me.

"Exactly. You were the one, after all, who calculated that, based on the people we know, a foreign woman's chances of being raped in one year in Ecuador are twenty-five percent. So two years in Ecuador raises your chances to forty-four percent."

"Thank you, math teacher." She paused. "But the thing is that I hate this country, but I love my kids."

"Jeannie, you don't love your kids. Okay, maybe you love your kids in that way a mother loves her wayward child, but you don't always like your kids. You spend a lot more time complaining about them than anything else. You hate how they steal from each other and kick each other's desks and talk out of turn. Every Tuesday you come home in the worst possible mood after teaching three Health classes back to back. Plus you're hoarse."

"Okay, Health is horrible," she admitted. "But the Madres always let second-years choose their schedules. I won't teach Health next year." She looked me right in the eye. "Maureen, I feel like leaving now would be abandoning them."

"But when you leave next year you'll still be abandoning them."

She raised an eyebrow, conceding the point. "I feel like I'm just now getting into the swing of things, figuring out how to teach, how to discipline, and now I'm leaving. I feel like I could be so much more effective next year and accomplish so many more things."

That Jeannie of all people should want to stay baffled me. But it angered me even more. I felt betrayed somehow, that we had commiserated together and raged against the corruption and the apathy and the domestic violence, that we had run a difficult course together and now, nearing the end, she was turning back and leaving me to go on alone, with no one to share my triumph at being able to repudiate it all, leave it all behind and move on to bigger and better and less depressing things. It seemed so completely illogical.

"Don't stay," I thundered, ticking off all of the reasons that she should leave: she could be the victim of a violent crime, the volunteers next year might not be very nice, the Madres might not let her accomplish any of her grand schemes, deferring her law school admission could be problematic, blah, blah, blah. She had an answer to every objection I raised, and an hour later, she was still resolute. "There's nothing you can say to make me change my mind," she said.

I went back to my room and got in bed, but sleep was elusive that night. I was still awake when the first rays of light began to penetrate my room, marveling at the changeability of the human character and the strength of the attachments we form.

CHAPTER SIXTEEN

You can tell a lot about a country by its prisons. In hippy-dippy Socialist Sweden, rapists and murders (all three of them) while away their days making arts and crafts in what are essentially taxpayer-funded mental health clinics. The Swedes' theory seems to be that a) anyone who commits such a crime must be crazy and b) with enough art therapy, the individual in question will soon become just another law-abiding, nude-sunbathing pot-smoker. In America, we think people in prison are either the victims of some terrible government conspiracy, the victims of "society"—whatever that means—or heinous evildoers. And if they are heinous enough, we fry them with electricity, unless of course they find Jesus first. The Swedes, in a nutshell, are tolerant and forgiving, verging on the naïve; Americans are religious and vengeful, suspicious of their government, and suckers for tear-jerking tales of redemption.

Three weeks before I arrived in Ecuador, I visited my first Latin American prison. It was in Bolivia, on a dusty street in downtown La Paz, tucked away behind a nondescript concrete façade. My guide was a German narco-trafficker named Hans who had figured out that he could make a fortune by charging morbidly curious backpackers ten dollars for a tour. Hans had piercing blue eyes and sunburned, leathery skin, and when an Australian woman asked him what he was going to do when he was released, he told us that he would go right back to narco-trafficking. "I've done a lot of recruiting during my time here," he explained in his odd guttural, clipped accent. "The next time around I'll be leading the operation, instead of being the stooge who gets caught."

Hans was a font of information. We learned that there was an average of a murder a month, that the guards could be bribed for just about anything, and that a kilo of cocaine was actually cheaper in the prison than it was on the street. Prisoners paid one boliviano (about thirteen cents) per day for lodging, and work was not an option, but a necessity: if you didn't work, you didn't earn money, and if you didn't earn money, you couldn't buy food. With its cobblers, photographers, and food vendors, the prison was a completely unregulated, largely self-contained economy that would have made Milton Friedman proud.

I was shocked to learn that whole families lived in the prison. At first I thought that I was imagining things, that the feminine features I saw peering out at us from the shadows were just clean-shaven teenage boys. But when I saw a silhouette with a distinctly "bread loaf" shape, as my politically incorrect high school Spanish teacher used to say, I asked Hans point-blank if there were women living in the prison.

"*Ja*, you can bring your wife to live with you if you pay one boliviano a day," Hans said, waving his arm dismissively as if this were a most uninteresting question. I couldn't imagine why any woman would want to come live here, but apparently there were quite a few who did. "And if you don't have one," he added, brightening, "they bring a busload of women from the women's prison every fifteen days."

"What if the women get pregnant?" the British woman next to me asked, frowning.

"Then they have a baby, and the baby lives with the mother at the women's prison. But if it's a boy, only until he's six. Then the child has to come live with his father here. Right now"—he pointed at a group of men across the courtyard, who were busy building a wall of cinderblock—"some of the prisoners are building a kindergarten."

But Hans saved his most interesting bit of trivia for the end of the tour, when we passed a soccer game in progress. Hans pointed at a large Coca-Cola billboard on the side of the canteen and explained that the company was the official sponsor of the prison soccer team. "That's pretty much the only rule in this place," he said without a trace of irony. "No Pepsi."

And so it was only natural that I wanted to visit an Ecuadorian prison. If my theory was correct and prisons were windows into a culture's worldview, I had to spend time in Latin American prisons if I was ever to understand Orlando and the millions of immigrants like him. But I suspected that what I had seen in Bolivia could have been an aberration. I had to have a sample size of at least two.

At ten o'clock in the morning on Mother's Day, Jeannie, Stacey, and I stood huddled beneath the awning of a fruit seller's stand, contemplating the concrete fortress of the Quito Women's Prison through the clammy drizzle. All around us, indigenous families crouched, babies strapped to their backs. Suddenly the crowd surged across the street, and we followed, eager to secure our place in line. "It'll probably just be a few minutes," I reassured the others, Pollyanna-like, as the drizzle turned to fat raindrops that pelted their cheeks. Stacey smiled weakly.

Leaning against the prison's barbed-wire topped concrete walls, I eavesdropped on the family behind us. They were Americans on a State Department-arranged trip to visit their daughter. A little blond girl, maybe ten or twelve years old, was with them, looking solemn and carefully carrying a large sheet cake with "Happy Mother's Day" scrawled across it in pink. I imagined the girl to be the inmate's daughter, her cherubic expression masking her role in the exquisitely planned and soon to be brilliantly executed prison break. I was sure that there was a saw in the cake.

The metal door swung open with the pomp of Ecuadorian officialdom. We stepped through the door into a concrete patio and were escorted into a concrete hut, where a woman sat at the desk checking passports and managing the guest sign-in log. When it was our turn, she asked whom we were there to see. "An American," I said.

"Sarah Patterson?"

"Oh, yes, that's the one," I lied. She jotted down "Sarah Patterson" and our passport numbers, confiscated our passports, and waved us through. Hoping to see the American family's ruse exposed, I lingered in the doorway, but the official didn't so much as dip her finger into the icing on the enormous cake. As she let them pass, I mentally prepared my dramatic first-person account of the escape for *CNN En Español*.

The minute we stepped through the doorway, however, I understood why the guard felt no need to inspect the cake. No one needed a saw to get out of this prison. As in Bolivia, inside there were no guards, no bars, no cells, and no dogs. Instead there was just a bunch of tough women living in a concrete three-story dormitory, hanging over the railings shouting across the patio at each other, bumming cigarettes off each other, and gossiping about who had Mother's Day guests and who didn't. "Do you know where we could find Sarah?" I asked the woman at the door.

"Hold on a minute," she said and raced off while a friend of hers escorted us into the patio to wait, which was not quite the way Stacey and Jeannie had envisioned it.

"I kind of imagined a solitary, machine-gun toting guard right there," Jeannie said as she pointed at the spectacle in the center of the patio. "Not so much."

In the place of Jeannie's armed guard there was...a DJ. Smack in the middle of the patio, beneath a makeshift canopy, he was spinning the Latin Top 40 while young women canoodled with their boyfriends—some no doubt the deadbeats who helped land them in jail in the first place—and admired their children. The single women danced provocatively, with long sidelong looks over their shoulders, and the many toothless, old indigenous women looked on passively.

The woman at the door returned a few minutes later. She didn't produce Sarah, but instead brought us a South African woman missing a few teeth. Apparently she thought any English-speaker was good enough. Pretty soon we had attracted a German and an American (not Sarah) as well. They told us that there were twenty-five more-or-less English-speaking prisoners there, all serving four-year sentences, half the sentence Ecuadorians receive for the same crime. "Four years," Jeannie joked. "You could really perfect your Spanish in that amount of time."

They looked at us blankly. "We don't talk to the Ecuadorian prisoners unless it's an absolute necessity," the South African explained. "So, no, our Spanish isn't really that good."

"What did you—how did you end up here?" I asked.

The German took a long drag on her cigarette and rolled her eyes. "Drug trafficking," she said, and the South African nodded.

"Me too," the baby-faced girl from Wyoming interjected. "I came here as an exchange student on the coast." None of them even bothered to pretend it had all been a mistake.

The German woman was the scariest of the three. Huge, menacing, and missing a lot of teeth, she was not someone I would ever want to meet in a dark alley at night. I asked what she did to stay busy, since apparently learning Spanish was not on her agenda. "Oh, I lead a dance troupe," she said, blowing smoke into my face.

"And you perform for the other inmates...?"

She stared at me as if I were the stupidest person she had ever met. "Of course not. All over Quito."

"I see," I exclaimed brightly, even though, in fact, I didn't. Quito seemed dangerous enough without the likes of her roaming the streets.

The South African nudged her friend and tapped her foot impatiently. She turned towards us. "Listen, there are some missionaries here having a party for Mother's Day with a cake and everything. Could you come back some other time?"

Jeannie handed them the presents we had brought—tampons and English-language magazines. Catching a glimpse of my tattered *Newsweek*s through the plastic bag, I cringed; it didn't seem like their type of reading material. "Next time you come, bring toilet paper," the German grumbled. "They don't provide it here." I nodded; now I knew what my Newsweek would be used for.

Summarily dismissed by the "English speaking" crew, there was nothing to do but return to the entrance and collect our passports. But while the others went on ahead, I lingered in the courtyard for a moment, mesmerized by the incongruity of a dance in prison yet struck by the similarities with the Valentine's Day dance I had organized. There were the petulant looks, the enamored couples, the bemused bystanders, the jealous bystanders, and the bored. The only thing missing was the boys cowering in the bathroom.

I wondered how many of my kids would end up at a prison dance one day, and whether life in prison would be much different from the lives they would or could lead on the "outside." The dormitories were of no worse construction than the kids' homes—in fact, maybe they were nicer. The entertainment was free, the missionaries brought cake, and the prisoners formed dance troupes. The prisoners didn't have toilet paper, but then neither did my kids.

I decided that Latin American governments did not intend for their prisons to be about punishment. Perhaps this was because punishment is expensive, and the state was broke. Perhaps this was because it was just too difficult to punish people whose lives were already pretty punishing and the way the West punishes prisoners—curbing their freedom—just doesn't make a lot of sense in a Latin American context. The truth was that most Latin Americans' freedom was already severely constrained by violence, political instability, and a seemingly never-ending downward spiral of economic hardship. There wasn't a lot more you could do to them.

It wasn't about rehabilitation either. It was nothing like Sweden's system, and it didn't even have America's half-hearted attempts at rehabilitation. There were no prison libraries, drug treatment centers, counseling sessions, job training programs, or literacy classes. Absolutely no services were provided at all, in fact, unless they were provided by the prisoners themselves or by visiting American missionaries.

What Latin American prisons had was a very simple mission: keep the criminals (or those taking the rap for the real criminals) separated from the rest of the population and do it in the very cheapest way possible. What happens within the prison walls is of little consequence.

In some ways, I had to admit that this approach had its merits. It was easy on the government's budget, to be sure, and as long as you didn't get murdered, had some means of bartering for food, and didn't get ill from the lack of hygiene, it was a comparably pleasant—and much less lonely—place to be imprisoned. It was almost cheerful, really. And whatever the prisoners lacked in formal education or training, the circumstances had forced them to become skillful entrepreneurs.

And it was, for better or for worse, just like the American penal system and the Swedish one, a microcosm of the society beyond its walls: every man for himself, and very few rules. Outside the walls, bus drivers don't have to pull over to the curb and doctors don't have to operate on dying children. Inside the walls, no one has to feed you. You're on your own. Just don't try ordering Pepsi.

CHAPTER SEVENTEEN

The driver peered into the rearview mirror at me. "Do you like Shakira?"

"Sure. I saw her in concert a few months back."

He turned up the volume until it sounded like Shakira was warbling "*Dónde están los ladrones?*" directly in my eardrum. "Lucky girl!" he shouted as he pounded on his horn and cut off a black SUV with tinted windows.

"I'll tell you where the *ladrones* are," he said without even missing a beat. "Here. In Guayaquil. Especially those damn Colombians. Guayaquil used to be a peaceful place. Then the U.S. started getting suspicious about ships arriving from ports in Colombia, so now they transport the stuff overland to Guayaquil and load it onto ships here. Mix it with legitimate cargo. Now you have turf wars. Drive-by shootings. Kidnappings at red lights." He lit a cigarette. "You've got your door locked, right?"

"Right," I squeaked as we swung around a corner and narrowly missed a kid on a bike. Gripped around the door handle, my knuckles were almost white.

"I hate those damn Colombians. Except for Shakira, of course. I'd marry her in a heartbeat. But the rest of them, forget it. We Ecuadorians have enough problems, without letting all of these Colombians come here. Of course we also have problems with our black people. They're a bunch of *ladrones* too. You have problems with black people in your country too, right?"

"Well, there is a fair amount of violence in the black community, which is very unfortunate. But that is because there is a lot of poverty—"

161

"Exactly."

I frowned, not wanting to offend him, seeing as how my life was quite literally in his hands. "Several of my friends were robbed at gunpoint by *mestizo* and indigenous Ecuadorians."

He raised an eyebrow. "How unusual."

Another taxi cut into his lane and he slammed on the brakes. "Crazy driver," he muttered and then looked back at me. "Other than that," he continued, "Guayaquil is a very beautiful city. Very modern. You'll like it."

The view from the window was not beautiful, however. Monochromatic in the extreme, it was a study in gray. A heavy gray smog hovered above the wide gray avenues lined with characterless gray buildings. Even the airport Hilton was a hideous gray monolith ringed with barbed wire. About the only splash of color was an occasional red neon sign heralding the entrance to yet another of the ubiquitous car dealerships.

We turned a corner and suddenly, out of nowhere, clusters of palatial homes in every pastel shade imaginable appeared before us. A pale green fortress loomed at the end of two long, straight rows of majestic palms, its carefully manicured lawn encircled by thick walls. Its neighbor was a dusty rose color, with faux Doric columns and an imposing black gate that gleamed in the midday sun. To me, it looked like a prison complex designed by Walt Disney.

My driver waved his hand dismissively. "See all this? It was all financed with drug money. Don't let anyone tell you anything different."

We veered off the main thoroughfare, and I became uneasy as endless blocks of villas sped past. Exceedingly residential, it seemed an unlikely route to what I imagined to be a shantytown-ringed campus.

Seemingly unnecessary detours by Ecuadorian taxi drivers always unnerved me. They unleashed my most paranoid thoughts and managed to remind me of every Latin American kidnapping/rape/murder horror story I had ever heard. With rising panic, I began to mentally review my self-defense moves. I decided that a vise-like grip around his neck, followed by a swift blow to the head, was my best bet. "Do you need to run some kind of errand?" I asked as nonchalantly as possible.

He looked at me quizzically in the rearview mirror. "No. We're going to *El Nuevo Mundo* school, just as you asked. In fact," he said as we pulled into a driveway, "this is it."

"It is?" I pressed my face to the window, my mouth hanging wide open. How could this possibly be an elementary and high school? The buildings were painted in bold pastels so unlike the Center's drab gray; the soccer fields had actual grass. The students wore smart new uniforms—much more fashionable, I thought, than the Catholic school uniforms I had worn as a child. They were more like prep school uniforms, with their cute plaid skirts, pressed khakis, and sporty V-necks. The students all looked like they should be playing lacrosse on the cover of a brochure for a small liberal arts college in California. "Are you sure?" I asked as a brand-new gymnasium came into view. It was covered, but the sides were open to the air, and it contained a brand-new volleyball court and rows upon rows of shiny bleachers.

"*Sí*," the driver reassured me as we came to a stop in front of a mission-style house. Tangles of vines crept up the cantaloupe-colored walls and onto the roof, and the small, fenced-in pool in the yard was a deep blue-green. "Good luck, *chica*, and remember, be careful!" he bellowed, hitting the gas. "Guayaquil is full of *ladrones!*"

The directors of *El Nuevo Mundo* had a wholly different business model than the Madres and Padre, and that was precisely the reason I had come. After eight months at the Center, I wasn't so sure that the Madres and Padre had all of the answers. We had no dedicated funding stream, which meant we often had to pay the teachers with IOUs. Without money to pay the teachers, we were unable to attract the quality of teachers that we needed to do what was admittedly a very tough job. Most of our students graduated with practical vocational skills, but almost no critical thinking ability and no leadership skills. They could barely read. As far as I was concerned, any of my kids could still wind up like Orlando, crammed into an empty gas tank en route to the American dream.

I suspected that, at its heart, our differences over methods really reflected the differences in our worldview. Perhaps it was just a reflection of my naiveté. I was, after all, a neophyte, while they had a combined ninety-five years of experience ministering to Ecuador's poor. Or perhaps the problem was that they were people of the cloth, and I was a mere mortal. They seemed to operate on two—and only two—mutually exclusive planes: the here and now of this world, and the spiritual ecstasy of the next. It would be fair, I think, to say that their favorite two philosophers were Adam Smith and Jesus Christ: they grimly prepared Ecuador's poor to survive this world—which they saw as a place in which most people's lives were nasty, brutal, and short—in the hopes that these humble people would achieve salvation in the afterlife of the Beatitudes. And in a way, this made perfect sense. What was the point, after all, of upending the social order of a world that was fleeting at best? And what difference will algebra make on Judgment Day? The Padre and the Madres operated on a micro level: they wanted to help this family make it through this year and they wanted to save their souls in the process. But they had no interest in helping Ecuador per se. That, they believed, was a lost cause.

But whatever the reason, the chasm was deep and wide. The directors of *El Nuevo Mundo*, I felt, might be the key to bridging the gap. They worked with children with the very same issues, and arguably worse. Between the two of them, they had spent almost as many years living in Ecuador; Renée was Ecuadorian by birth. And they had been nuns in the very same order as the Madres. The reasons for their departure were a bit murky, but after hearing the basic premise behind their school—arming the poor of Guayaquil with the same top-notch liberal arts education afforded to the city's wealthiest families—I sensed that perhaps, despite the Madres' obvious continuing affection for them, it had come down to a difference of philosophy. It seemed as though they intended for the poor to inherit *this* earth.

"In the morning," Renée explained as we sat munching on plantain chips in the kitchen, "we use the campus as a for-profit school for the children of wealthy families." She was petite, with expressive dark eyes and a hearty laugh, and she had the endearing habit of occasionally reaching over and squeezing my wrist as she spoke. She made me feel as if I had known her for years even though we had just met.

"The profits," Mary, her white-haired American counterpart, interjected, "are used to subsidize the afternoon school for poor children." Because of this arrangement, she explained, only twenty-five percent of the funding for the afternoon school came from donations. An added benefit was that the poor children had the same top-notch teachers and facilities—including brand-new science and computer labs—as Guayaquil's elite.

"Almost all of our poor children go to college," Renée said proudly. "We even have a few studying on scholarship in the United States."

"My kids can barely read," I groused. "I can't imagine any of them going to college in the States."

Renée patted my arm and reminded me that *El Nuevo Mundo* had an entrance exam. "That makes a big difference," she said gently. It was true, but somehow I wasn't consoled. Entrance exam or not, they were still preparing hundreds of kids for professions in education, law, medicine, and government, while I was preparing kids for a lifetime of dyeing old women's hair purple and retooling old cars.

I asked Renée if I could sit in on a few classes, and she obliged. The first was a ninth-grade Spanish class. Upon entering the classroom, the students went to their desks, pulled out a notebook and a pen, and quietly waited for the teacher to arrive. When she entered the classroom, they stood at attention and then sat in their seats, no one kicking or punching each other, or casting sidelong looks at members of the opposite sex, or staring vacantly at the ceiling. They nearly leapt out of their seats each time the teacher gave them an opportunity to participate, and I seethed with jealousy as I looked out at the sea of raised hands. Why weren't my kids like this?

The fourth-grade math class I went to was much the same. The nine and ten-year-olds knew fractions better than my twelve-to-sixteen year-old boys did, and no one proposed to the attractive young teacher or whistled at her. The chalkboard was smooth and saliva-free; the floor was smooth and polished. She didn't seem to have any kind of discipline system, and she didn't seem to need one. I wondered what she would say if I told her that I spent most of my Saturdays supervising the cleaning of the boys' bathroom.

Later that afternoon, I accompanied Renée on a visit to the shantytown in which most of the students lived. Climbing into the backseat, I squeezed in between two women who were hitching a ride with us; they were parents of children at the school. While Renée chatted up front with the driver, our pick-up truck whizzed through traffic, past the glitzy malls and the pink and yellow and

165

baby blue mansions, crossed the wide expanse of the river, and then spit us out into a shantytown of winding dirt tracks along its banks. Tiny black children peered out at us from one-room reed shacks while their mothers traced designs in the dirt with their bare feet. The only things that seemed to be moving in this area of town were the mosquitoes.

We pulled up to large, freshly painted pink building, by far the nicest building in the neighborhood. "This," Renée said as we piled out of the truck, "is one of our pre-schools." The intent of the pre-school, she explained, was to prepare the neighborhood children for *El Nuevo Mundo*. Inside, the children looked just the same as the ones outside. The stark difference was their surroundings: puzzles and alphabet letters rather than mud and mosquitoes.

Renée led me across a courtyard and into the sewing shop, one of the many businesses they had started to provide a means of employment and job training for neighborhood residents. Busy at work on their machines, the women paused to proudly display the baby clothes they had made that morning. A broad woman with pockmarked skin shyly held out a red gingham jumper for my inspection. "*Bonito, no?*"

"*Muy bonito,*" I replied and she broke into a grin.

Taking me by the arm, Renée led me past yards of purple checks, pink polka dots, and blue pinstripes, dispensed advice about fabric to buy and items to sew, and showered praise on the workers. "Last week the boys' clothes didn't sell so well," she gently reminded the women. "Try making more girls' clothes. And use less lace—it's expensive." Then we were off again.

As we jolted up and down on the deeply rutted road, I reflected on just how different this shantytown was than the ones in Quito. It was startling, really. Geographically speaking, we were only two hundred miles away, but in many ways we seemed thousands of miles away. There was a lot less commerce and a lot more flowers. Instead of poplars, there were palms. Instead of the solid concrete buildings, there were fragile-looking huts of wood and thatch. It even smelled different—the pleasant aroma of spices and mangoes mingled with the less salubrious odor of raw sewage, which was pretty much all you could smell in Quito's poorer quarters. So absorbed was I in my own ruminations that I didn't realize something was wrong until one of the women with us interrupted to ask Renée if we should go to the police station.

And then I saw them. Not fifty feet behind us, a man was wildly waving a gun and screaming at a young woman while a crowd gathered behind them. The frequency and intensity of the crowd's outbursts mirrored the intensity of the scene unfolding, and one sensed that there were two camps: those squarely in the woman's camp and those egging on her husband.

The more desultory onlookers lounged on the sidelines. Oblivious to all of the commotion, a toddler in a faded yellow T-shirt dangled from his mother's arms, sliding his feet through the rust-colored grit. She stood perfectly still, her gaze fixed on the cowering woman in silent witness. Her expression was enigmatic to say the least. I could not tell if the woman was her friend, her sister, or just a woman she passed by on the way to the bus stop.

"He's going to kill her," one of my backseat companions remarked in a dull monotone. It sounded as though she had seen this before.

We watched in horror as the man roughly grasped the woman's chin and yanked her cheek within an inch of his own. As he raised the shiny barrel to her temple, I held my breath. From our vantage point, their cries were unintelligible and their expressions somewhat muted, but even so the sense of fear and loathing was palpable. He shouted something, his fleshy lips a hair's breadth from her face. She jerked her face away. Was it instinctive fear or a twitch of revulsion? Had his eyelashes brushed her cheek, reminding her of how that had felt in better times? Was she reeling from a whiff of his stale whiskey breath? And then they stood motionless, silhouetted against a crimson sky, locked in a silent dialogue of past wrongs, real and imagined. I hoped that it was all for show, but somehow I doubted it.

Indignation flashed across Renée's features, and she dug her fingernails into the dashboard. "To the police station. Hurry." She instructed the driver in a low, steely voice, and wordlessly, he obeyed.

The police station was a one-room concrete bunker tucked away on side street riddled with potholes. "*Policía*" was inscribed on the façade in big block letters, and a badly faded mural adorned the side. The only signs of human habitation were a few rusting Coke cans littering the yard.

Renée hurried into the station, and we sat in awkward silence. Craning his neck, the driver peered through the windshield. "There's no patrol car here," he observed.

"Or police," the woman on my left added, smoothing her skirt with her long coffee-colored fingers. "Do you think we should take him in our truck?" She nervously gestured towards the building's solitary window. Through heavy metal bars we watched Renée argue with the lone dispatcher

The other woman shook her head vigorously. "Are you crazy? Then this guy will just kill us too. We'd be snitches."

I tuned out of the conversation. It was all too surreal debating the odds of our survival, our place in an endless cycle of retribution; destiny appeared cruelly disposed to the soft of heart. Allow someone to be killed, or intervene and be killed. Kill or be killed. I thought of Charles Darwin. He had developed his theory of evolution during his sojourn on Ecuador's remote Galápagos Islands, where he found the torpid and sexually inept tortoise living out its two-hundred-year-old lifespan in splendid isolation, safe from the depredations of the more fleet-of-foot and virile predators that had rendered their ancient mainland cousins extinct. Now I felt like a modern Darwin myself, observing how humans preserve their gene pool: by keeping their mouth shut and minding their own business. I morbidly pondered whether human evolution was one long race to the bottom that rewarded the brutish, the docile, and the emotionally deadened.

Renée emerged from the police station at last. Looking tired and drawn, she slammed the truck door shut and faced us with a forced, tight-lipped smile. "He radioed a nearby patrol car. It's the best we can do."

"Do you think anyone will actually come?"

She shrugged and looked out the window. "Maybe."

We dropped the women off at their homes and sped out of the shantytown, a cloud of dust trailing behind us. When the bumpy jolting transitioned to the smooth whirring of rubber on pavement, I breathed a sigh of relief. The sky turned scarlet, then lavender, and finally deep violet. One by one, the corner stores switched their electric lights on. I rolled down the window and stuck my head out, suddenly acutely attuned to the slightest nuances of human interaction, the sights and sounds and smells that seemed to press in from every direction. A fishmonger and his wife packed up their wares for the night. A boy on a bike waved at me. Two girls linked arms and skipped down the street.

At last we swung into Nuevo Mundo's driveway. In the glare of the headlights, one of the guards shielded his eyes and ran towards us. He rapped on the driver's window impatiently. *"Ayúdenme!"* he shouted. *"Ayúdenme !"* He told us that he had just received a call from his wife, who was gravely ill and had been taken to the hospital downtown. Mary had offered to drive him, but not until we returned; she was afraid of driving in the city alone at night.

Within minutes, we piled into Mary's van and headed out. Renée gave Mary directions from the backseat, while the guard alternately stared straight ahead and chattered nervously about his wife. "It's probably nothing, right?" he said to no one in particular. "She's probably imagining things. Sometimes women do, you know. But she has been vomiting a lot lately, and she has a high fever...."

Renée tapped Mary's shoulder. "Here. This is the exit."

The ramp dead-ended in an older section of town. Palms rustled in the sultry evening breeze, and the air was redolent with briny fish and raw sewage; the faint mustiness of river water mingled with the brackishness of the sea. At the first stoplight, a brunette in a short pink dress and fishnet stockings stood in a dimly lit entryway, smoking. Ringed with dark make-up, her eyes looked like cigarette burns in an olive-brown carpet. A passing drunk leered at her, but she appeared not to even notice as she lifted her heel to let a rat scurry by. Mary tapped the 'lock' button.

We made a sharp turn and the guard alighted in front of a crumbling blue façade with a line a block long stretching out the door. I glanced at Mary. "Why don't they go in the waiting room?"

She regarded me with a look that was half-sad, half-amused. "This is the waiting room," she said. "Sometimes you wait for hours, maybe even days. And once you are inside, you might wait a few days more. One friend of ours went in with a leg wound, and they left him lying on the floor for three days without even washing the wound. He lost his leg as a result."

I hoped the same fate did not await the guard's wife. As we sped away, I peered out at the faces of those in line. Some were ghastly pale or contorted in pain, while others were placid and serene, resigned to their fate. But none registered the irony that here in the remnant of the Inca Empire, where doctors had successfully performed brain surgery five hundred years ago, it now took three days to see a mediocre physician.

A head, a torso, an arm: that's all there was to the first man I laid eyes on at Sister Susie's leper hospital, my last stop in Guayaquil. The left side of his face had a giant cavity, and his left eye was swollen shut. The right one was a strange robin's egg-blue. Balanced on a low stool just a few inches from the ground, he ran the thick hammock threads between his scaly thumb and forefinger, then expertly curled the threads around his forefinger and into a knot. Over and over, he measured, yanked, and knotted in an elegant syncopated rhythm: slow, quick, quick, slow, quick, quick. Within a matter of minutes, he had tied dozens of knots, each appearing to be exactly the same distance apart.

Further down the line, his armless colleague had quite a different technique. Resting his shoulder blades against the wall, his torso and his outstretched legs formed a perfect "V" shape. With the toes on right foot, he measured the fibers. Then, he yanked the threads between his first and second toe, wrapped them around his right foot's big toe, and with a final tug, secured the knot.

Invisible to them all, I stood on the edge of this forest of wooden beams, peering through thick webs of silvery fibers, a silent voyeur. Most of the men's skin was covered in red, white, and gray boils. From a distance, it looked like they were covered in mold.

Even though I had been forewarned about the patients' condition, it was jarring nonetheless to see lepers in real life. I associated leprosy with miracles of Biblical proportion, bell-ringing outcasts of the Middle Ages, and leprosariums on isolated tropical atolls; I did not associate the disease with a modern colony of hammock artisans tucked away in a warren of industrial warehouses.

Hansen's disease was its new, modern name, after Dr. G. H. Armauer Hansen of Norway, who first identified the bacteria that caused the disease in 1873. Previously, it had been considered a hereditary disease, a curse, or even a punishment from God; medieval lepers were required to wear special identifying clothing, carry clappers and bells to warn of their approach, and walk on the designated side of the street. Some medieval scholars believed that those suffering from leprosy were experiencing purgatory on earth;

one medieval monk reportedly prayed fervently to contract the disease in the hopes of attaining salvation through extreme suffering, and eventually his prayers were answered. This tradition persisted even into the nineteenth century: one of the most famous names in the annals of leprosy is the saintly Father Damien, who founded a leper colony on the remote Hawaiian island of Molokai and eventually succumbed to the disease himself. Sister Susie had named the hospital Damien House in his honor.

Dr. Hansen's great contribution was to lift the disease out of its mystical, morality-laden context and into the realm of science. Researchers began to explore the mechanism of transmission, as well as treatment options. What they eventually found, Sister Susie had informed me with her wide smile and expressive dark eyes, was that Hansen's disease was actually one of the least contagious of all infectious diseases. Although transmitted by droplets from the nose and mouth, the risk of contagion was exceedingly low unless one was in close and continuing contact with an untreated, infected individual. Those who had suffered from Hansen's disease but had received or were receiving treatment were not contagious.

The legless, one-armed man paused and dropped his threads. He gingerly reached down and placed his hand on the floor, then hoisted his torso off of the stool. Balanced upon a single hand, he hopped in my direction.

I stumbled backwards to avoid a collision, and my leg pounded into something hard and smooth. A dry, reptilian surface brushed my elbow. "Who's there? Who's there?" a loud voice cried out from behind.

I spun around and saw that I had backed into a small wooden table, at which two men were playing dominoes. The reptilian-like surface was an arm, and I shuddered as I stared at the withered limb; it felt as though I had been touched by death itself.

"Maureen," I mumbled, unsure what to say.

"What? Who are you?"

I cleared my throat. "My name is Maureen," I said a little louder. "I am visiting from Quito. I work at the _____ Center."

"Aha!" the older of the two domino players said appreciatively. "The Center in Quito. I have heard good things about it."

"You want to play, young lady?" his companion asked me, slurring his words through his twisted mouth, and pointing a bony

171

index finger in the general direction of my voice. I ducked instinctively as his arm swung closer to my face.

"*Sí,*" I said in my bravest sounding voice.

He broke into a broad grin. "My partner and I are going to beat you badly. We're pretty good. Probably get a little more practice than you." His deformed chest cavity shook with laughter, and soon his friend joined in.

"We're not laughing at you," his friend explained. "Just having a good time. We love having visitors. Where are you from?"

"The United States."

"George Boosh!" shouted one.

"Mickey Mouse!" shouted the other.

They couldn't think of anything else they knew about America, so they dissolved into laughter again. For a couple of guys missing their sight, their teeth, half of their faces, and a couple of limbs, they sure seemed happy. Suddenly I felt guilty for all of the times I had wallowed in self-pity. At least I had all of my fingers and toes.

They explained the rules to me, and I discovered that I definitely did not know how to play dominoes. I had always thought all you did was match the numbers up, but apparently that was not the case. The one on my left coached me on the sly, feeling the raised dots on the domino with the stubby fingers on his one arm. Then he would hold up the one that I should use and place it back down on the table. And even though I knew it wasn't contagious, each time I found myself just barely touching the sides of the domino as I slid it into place. I rationalized that since neither one of them could see, I wasn't really obliged to show just how brave and tolerant I was. As far as they knew, I was licking them between moves.

I was saved from ignominious defeat by the church bells. The Mass was a joyous affair. Every time there was a musical interlude—about every five minutes—the residents banged on their drums and tambourines as if they hadn't a care in the world, hadn't lost their limbs and their sight and their families and their homes. Sister Susie stood in the front pew and swayed with the music. In her late forties, she had thick salt-and-pepper hair that went all the way down to her waist. During each prayer, she clasped hands with the residents without the slightest flinch, and during one she even curled her fingers between one resident's gnarled toes. Inspired by Sister Susie, I swallowed hard and grasped the three fingers of the woman next to me. It's not that bad, I told myself, as I felt the panic rising in my throat. Look at Sister Susie. She's been hugging and touching people with leprosy for years and looks like the perfect picture of health. Just pretend that you are touching someone with an awful lot of calluses. And to my surprise, as long as I didn't actually look at her hand, it worked.

After Mass, Sister Susie took me on a tour. We stopped at the "room" of each resident—a bed separated from the next with a sheet hung for privacy—briefly. Each resident had learned a craft and spent his or her time producing handicrafts for sale to visitors. While the men sewed hammocks in the patio, the women made dolls and Christmas ornaments in their "rooms". One woman shyly showed us the angel ornaments she had made. I watched as her charred fingers skimmed the angel's smooth brown face; thick scars from third-degree burns covered her face, neck, and arms. "Her neighbors set fire to her hut and tried to burn her alive," Sister Susie explained to me in a low voice. "That's how afraid people are of catching it."

In the next room, Isabel, a small, gray-haired woman in a bright red jogging suit, described years of gradually worsening symptoms as she clutched my hand tightly. "For four years, I gradually lost sensation in my hands and feet," she explained. "Then one day I had a ball on my leg that was hard and black." She cupped her hands in a sphere the size of an orange and looked down, embarrassed. She spoke so low that I had to move in closer to hear her. "I thought maybe a bug had bit me, maybe some kind of worm was burrowed beneath my skin."

"Did you go to the doctor?" I asked gently.

Isabel looked confused. It was the same look Hot William has given me when I asked whether his mom had taken his baby sister to the hospital before she died. "No," she said, shaking her head. "But I took a razor from my master's house and sliced open the big black ball to see what it was, but I couldn't see anything."

I shuddered. I couldn't imagine doing anything like that. In my family, we wince when we get a shot. We wouldn't sink a razor into a bubbling patch of possibly worm-infested flesh in a million years.

But Isabel did not seem to find anything particularly interesting or unusual in this part of her story, and she continued on. "I began to suffer from high fevers," she whispered, squeezing my hand tighter. "My body was wracked with pain and the skin on my feet split open. My friends just said I had ugly feet, and the doctor gave me pills that did nothing. Nobody suspected I had leprosy."

Isabel began to weep, brushing the tears away with the back of her hand. "One day I was at my friend's house grinding and roasting cocoa beans to make chocolate all day and when I got home I realized that I had burned my whole knee off and I didn't even know it." From what Sister Susie had told me earlier, incidents like this were apparently quite common. Often the greatest problems stemmed not from the disease itself, but from the accidents that were exacerbated by the individual's lack of sensation. Unlike a healthy person, who would seek some sort of assistance after sustaining an injury—or at the very least scream until someone came and helped him or her—people with leprosy have no idea that they even need help, and the lack of treatment can have serious consequences.

"The wound didn't heal for over a year and a half," Isabel said, "until a woman told me to go into the jungle and find a tree that releases milk; I put this on my knee as ointment and it was healed. But the fevers just kept getting worse, and one day while cleaning my master's house, I went into a deep sleep."

"What she means is a coma," Sister Susie whispered in my ear.

"And when I woke up," Isabel said brightly, the gleam suddenly returning to her bright, dark eyes, "I was here with Sister Susie."

"You certainly are lucky," I said.

"*Sí*," she said. Her thin lips parted in a smile, showing three crooked, yellow teeth. It wasn't the kind of smile you see on a poster at the orthodontist, but it was lovely nonetheless.

The next woman we visited had arguably suffered even worse—fevers, migraines, hallucinations. "The people in the village thought that someone had cast a spell on me," she recounted in a hoarse whisper. She wore a bright floral housedress and had curlers in her hair. "They took me to a witch doctor and he made me bathe my legs in boiling milk, which burned my legs badly. I didn't know it at the time, though, because I didn't have any sensation in my legs." She squeezed Sister Susie's hand. "I tried many treatments, but nothing worked. I even tried to kill myself twice."

"And aren't you glad you didn't succeed?" Sister Susie asked in her cheeriest voice.

The woman nodded vigorously. "*Muy agradecida*," she agreed.

Sister Susie and I returned to the patio, and I dutifully gave my two domino-playing friends a good-bye hug, trying not to cringe. Sister Susie smiled approvingly.

"*Adiós, mi amiga!*" the younger one shouted as I extricated myself from the embrace. "Go back to Quito and practice. Maybe next time you will win."

His friend's message was quite a bit more serious. "Sister Susie," he whispered in my ear, "is an angel sent by God."

He was right, of course. She was an angel, or at the very least a saint. But she was more than just a martyr to me. She was a beacon of hope, and in a strange way, she and Renée and Mary brought me closer to the Padre and the Madres than I had ever been in Quito. In two days I had seen the best of human nature and the worst. I had seen the saints among us win some and lose some. But despite overwhelming odds, they had never given up.

CHAPTER EIGHTEEN

A couple of weeks before school ended, I had a hot date with Hot William. It wasn't really a date *per se*, but in my head, of course, it was. After all, as Jeannie put it, "How many times are you going to have the chance to go out with a guy with the word 'hot' in his name? If he asked you to go dancing with him, I think you can count it, fair and square."

Our rendezvous point was a patch of crumbling sidewalk half a block up the hill from the Center. Across from the local video shack, which proudly displayed posters for Sylvester Stallone movies and pornos, it was hardly a romantic spot. It was, however, a very strategic one: we couldn't be seen from the Center. The Madres had imposed a strict dating ban on the volunteers.

Hot William was waiting for me when I arrived. He was wearing his best clothes—a pair of new, white nylon track pants, the only thing he owned that wasn't a hand-me-down—and his huge white grin glinted in the darkness. "*Adónde vamos?*"

We debated the merits of various destinations for a few minutes and finally decided to take a bus to Amazonas—otherwise known as *Gringolandia*—where there would be numerous clubs from which to choose. "Wow," Hot William kept saying as we walked down Amazonas. "Wow!" He was amazed to discover how many clubs were packed into this small area, and even more amazed to see the throngs of wealthy Ecuadorians streaming in and out of the swanky clubs, the women sparkling in slinky sequined tops and the men looking suave and bored in their designer jeans and shiny black shoes. I cringed as I watched a bouncer approvingly look over a

176

brunette with long curly hair and six-inch spike heels, suddenly realizing that getting Hot William past Amazonas' cadre of power-hungry, fashion-conscious gatekeepers might be more difficult than I had thought.

We passed the English pub favored by the volunteers, with its cozy booths, pool tables, and dark paneled wood; No-Bar, a dark den of licentiousness that seemed to exert an odd magnetic force on the volunteers; a few foreboding façades booming techno music; and several "beach bar"-type establishments, in which sunburned Australian and British backpackers sipped fruity drinks in a completely incongruous tropical setting. We walked in silence, smiling nervously at each other each time we made eye contact, but suddenly unable to think of a single thing to say. "Are you hungry?" Hot William finally asked.

"A little." I tried to be noncommittal, mindful of the fact that he had little money, yet would probably feel obligated to pay no matter what I said. The truth was that I was starving, not having eaten since lunch. It was now ten o'clock.

Hot William suggested that we get a bite to eat, and I wracked my brain for a cheap option, which was difficult. Amazonas was gringo central, and everything was priced for tourists and the rich Ecuadorians who wanted to imitate them. Finally I remembered a Lebanese take-out counter a few blocks away. For a mere two dollars, the humorless owner would hack off a slab of glistening gyro meat, throw it on a paper plate, douse it in tzatziki sauce, and fling it across the counter at you. It wasn't service with a smile, but it was fast, cheap, and hygienic. The volunteers loved it, especially after a long night of drinking.

At the counter, Hot William graciously asked if I would like something to drink and I shook my head. In reality I was dying for a mango lassi, but I was worried that he would insist on paying. I couldn't justify spending his whole family's daily food budget on what was essentially just a little fruit-flavored yogurt.

And just as I suspected, when I reached into my purse for cash, Hot William steadfastly refused my offer to pay. "Wow! A woman who wants to pay," he exclaimed, smiling and waving my dollars away. "Don't be ridiculous." Even so, I felt him wince as he handed four crumpled dollars to the man. There goes a whole day's pay, I thought.

We walked along narrow streets flush with gaudy neon lights and beautiful, half-naked people, devouring our sandwiches as we walked, tzatziki sauce streaming down our chins. Finally, we came to a small square with a cast-iron fountain and sat on a bench. Close but not too close.

"What do you want to do with the rest of your life?" Hot William asked as he licked some sauce off of his fingers.

"I don't know."

"You have to come up with something," he insisted.

"Okay. Be a Renaissance woman."

Hot William looked confused. "What does that mean?"

"You know, someone who tries a lot of things. I want to hike the Appalachian Trail and be mayor of some town and be a famous author."

He laughed. "Wow! What kind of books are you going to write?"

"All kinds. I'm writing a book about Ecuador right now."

"You are? Really?"

"Really."

"Am I in it?"

"Do you want to be in it?"

"Absolutely! Are you kidding? And be sure to use my real name. I want everyone to know that I, William Rojas, am just a poor Ecuadorian, a graduate of the Center, but that I am going to be President of Ecuador someday! Write that! *Presidente de la República del Ecuador!*" He clearly relished the sound of that. "Oh, and lie a little and say I'm really handsome."

"You don't need to worry about that. I have that covered. Did you know all of the volunteers call you Hot William?"

He was confused for a moment by my translation, not quite sure what a *William Caliente* was. "You know, sexy," I said.

He broke into a big grin and laughed. "Are you serious?"

"Completely."

"This ugly face? That's funny." I shrugged and he laughed again. "Where to now, famous author?"

I thought for a moment and remembered a club that I had seen near the Center—a postage stamp-sized entryway of threadbare carpet and a stairwell leading down into the building's cellar. It was probably a whole lot cheaper than the clubs lining Amazonas. "Cotocollao, *Señor Presidente.*" I saluted him and his picked me up, threw me on his back, and took me on a dizzying piggy-back ride down Amazonas.

Drunk on life and its possibilities, we careened down the avenue, two idealists ready to take on the world. The street was cool now in the damp of the evening, the signs for locksmiths and tourist trinkets and pharmacies gone dark. It was the same route I had taken on that strange bus ride home from the Panecillo a few months back, and yet everything was different. The passengers on that bus had filled me with despair that anything would ever be different, that they would ever be other than docile, illiterate peasants, cogs in a system they could neither comprehend nor hope to improve; Hot William had quite the opposite effect on me. They could not read the signs as we sped along and had no use for them anyway; Hot William could read every one.

We raced past a travel agency advertising cheap flights to the Galápagos, a bakery, and a corner store. The sidewalk sped by, faster and faster, and with each thud I tightened my grip around Hot William's neck. It was frightening and exhilarating all at the same time, like riding a horse that hadn't been broken.

"I'm going to own this store one day," Hot William crowed as we dashed past a furniture store.

"I know!" I shouted and somehow, as we galloped off into the night, I did.

An unexpected emotion hit me my last few weeks in Ecuador: sorrow. After all of the hours I had spent wishing to be anywhere else than this godforsaken country, where life was cheap and truth elusive, all of evenings I had whiled away in my room reading European novels in an escapist flight of fancy from the mounds of illegible and nearly illiterate essays strewn about my floor, and all of the abuse I had heaped on Ecuador, I actually felt a wave of nostalgia for the Center, for the kids, wayward as they might be, and even for Quito.

I first felt it in when my ninth-graders left school a few weeks early to begin their vocational internships. As I gave my standard, not all that inspired "it was a pleasure to teach you speech," tears welled up in my eyes. "Don't cry, Maureen," one of my students said in that voice that one uses when reasoning with an overly dramatic toddler.

We headed out onto the soccer field for a class picture and a raucous soccer game. When it was over, I slipped away quietly to avoid any more pathetic good-byes. As long as I didn't have to talk to any of the kids, or God forbid, hug them, I would be just fine. I sprinted up the steps to the teachers' lounge, with one of the carpentry boys in hot pursuit. "Teacher, teacher," he called after me. I finally had to acknowledge him and turn around. He shook my hand vigorously and tearfully thanked me for all the hours I had put in tutoring him so he could pass. I should have talked longer with him, but I couldn't. Instead I wished him the best of luck and dashed into the teachers' lounge, mercifully off limits to students.

Several of the ninth-graders kept dropping by the Center after that. Many had enrolled in the Center's night school program, which began a week after their classes ended. "We don't understand anything the new Spanish teacher says," they whined every time they saw me. "Maybe *gringos* just make better Spanish teachers." I told them to stop being ridiculous and pay more attention in class, maybe then they would learn something, but of course secretly I was flattered.

My sixth grade girls were another story. Cristina and Carmen were not too sad to see me go—somehow I didn't think they'd be harassing their English teacher next year to be more like me—but Dolores clung to me mournfully as I trudged down the steps to the bus stop one last time. "I'll miss you," she mumbled. Her face was streaked with dirt, and her blue-black hair was hopelessly tangled. It didn't look like she'd taken a bath or changed her clothes in days. For a while it had seemed that her family situation had improved somewhat, but lately it seemed to have deteriorated again.

"Cheer up," I said, determined to put the best possible spin on things. "You'll be in junior high next year. You'll have new *gringos*. They'll take you on fieldtrips to McDonald's and take you to ride the escalators."

"Maybe," she said, her voice quavering, but she didn't sound too convinced.

One day not long before the end of school, I came across Eduardo, one of the kids who had been kicked out of my Math class, on the steps outside the Madres' office. I sat down beside him and inquired what he was up to. "Working," he replied glumly.

"And I bet you miss me, don't you?" I joked.

To my surprise, he just nodded solemnly. "What are you teaching in class?"

I pulled out the textbook and let him flip through it while I painted a rosy picture of the world of geometry and proportional fractions. His eyes widened when I described playing Math Blaster on the computers in the library. He looked very impressed, very unlike the Eduardo that I knew.

Saying good-bye to his classmates was by far the hardest part. On the last day of school, I limped out to the soccer field with them, weighed down by the boys clinging to every available limb. Stacey walked along beside us, intent on taking one last photo of me and my boys. "Couldn't we trade you for Stacey?" they asked. "You know, she goes and you stay."

I looked over at Stacey. She didn't seem too offended. "No," I said. "It is time for me to go home."

We assembled ourselves on the field and Stacey took our picture. I ran inside the volunteer house, grabbed my tennis shoes, and changed my shoes on the sidelines as the game began. I made one glorious goal—my first ever. But even such intense concentration on the task at hand did not keep the tears from flowing. By the end of the game, I was a sorry mess. Each one gave me a solemn hug and demanded I come back and visit. Darwin took out a pen and scrawled my phone number in the States across his arm.

"It's too expensive to call," I said.

"How much does it cost?"

"Maybe twenty cents a minute."

"Oh, that's nothing," he assured me. Yeah right, I thought, a fifteen-minute call is a whole day's wage for you. I knew he and his classmates wouldn't call, but it was nice to hear nonetheless.

I asked the boys to write down their addresses, but nobody had an address. Dumb me. I had lived in Ecuador long enough to know that. The post office doesn't deliver to shantytowns. So they wrote down their names and the street they lived on, if it had a name, or if it didn't, the name of their shantytown. After their name, most wrote, "I love you. You are my favorite teacher," or something very similar.

I never knew that they could be so expressive.

EPILOGUE

I may have left Ecuador, but it did not leave me. It was a silent stalker, a jealous lover who refused to be forgotten, a spirit that lurked in the deepest reaches of my soul. It was a voice inside my head that commanded me to look in the store windows and see who was following me, that made me jump when a Hispanic man harmlessly whistled at me and made an admiring comment about my *culo* to his gold-toothed companion, that made me suspicious of the slightest act of human kindness. It was with me whenever I saw a child scamper in front of a bus or a car and held my breath until he made it across. It was with me in the dead of the night, when unseen attackers held me down and the man in the dusty street in Guayaquil at last pulled the trigger and the lepers beat tambourines and Edison shined shoes until I woke up, sweating profusely and clutching my pillow. It was with me at school, whenever I overheard a classmate in my MBA program whine that he couldn't get by on an $80,000 a year salary in New York, and I wanted to scream and ask him just why he felt so entitled.

It was the white noise that filled my ears every time I rode the subway or strolled through the city or was anywhere at all that I found myself people-watching, oblivious to everything else, caught up in wondering who their Ecuadorian counterpart was. Was the successful young consultant with his briefcase and his silk tie and his cell phone Hot William in better circumstances? Or did the circumstances make Hot William who he was? Did I see Darwin in the angry young man with the gold chains around his neck or the well-dressed young man cuddling with his girlfriend while they

182

waited for the train? I sat there and mused, and I wondered if they realized just how lucky they were.

It was with me too when I found myself on a beach with a Colombian man I barely knew, telling him about the day Oscar died and unexpectedly bursting into tears. He droned on and on about the inscrutability of God's plans and how I should not despair, that I must have made a difference no matter how small, and while I know that he only intended to comfort me, it infuriated me instead. I did not see God in any of what happened to Oscar, and I was not crying for myself. I was crying for everyone else who did not cry, who did not see how tragic the life and death of Oscar and a thousand like him had been. I cried for Edison and his mute, terrorized sisters and the little girl who asked me how much a prostitute earned. I cried for the little girls and boys whose names were solemnly pulled out of the cardboard box and read at Mass every week. I cried for the "peasants"—the once nameless, faceless mob that was now composed of people I knew, of Marías and Carmens and Antonios and Edisons. When the newspaper said they rioted and then went home, I could now picture what they went home to, and it wasn't pretty.

It had begun as a quest for knowledge, but far from ending when I left the country, it morphed into a quest for understanding. For me, Ecuador was no longer a wedge on the map. It had become a state of mind, a terrifying reminder of how thin the veneer of civilization really is, a symbol of how easily it can be stripped away. For me, the word "Ecuador" had become a kind of shorthand for something that transcended time and place: a grinding, soul-sapping poverty of body, mind, and spirit. It existed anytime and anywhere human misery was accepted as the way things are, have been, and always will be. It was anywhere and everywhere fatalism reigned, where the future was just one long tunnel to the past, where the poor were relegated to lives totally consumed by the details of survival and the rich to vapid lives lived behind high walls and barbed wire. It was anywhere a group's sense of rights and obligations began to break down and the law of the jungle took over. It was corruption, and it was greed. It was the dark side of the human soul. And it had even become, if I dared to admit it, the dark side of me.

Why did "Ecuador" even still exist, I wondered? Economists and politicians were forever telling us that we were living in a new modern era, that democracy was sweeping the globe, that literacy rates were soaring, that globalization was bringing not only new products but also new ideas to every corner of the planet, that a new "global consensus" had emerged. Nearly everyone, they assured us, agreed that the path to peace and prosperity lie in participatory democracies, protection for the rights of the individual, the rule of law, the flourishing of civil society, and open markets. And in a sense, my own informal research had borne this out: Ecuadorians said they wanted all of these things. But they also said they wanted an American President; they didn't have faith in the ability of their own leaders to bring this about.

Could it be, I wondered, that even in a so-called modern era, we remain prisoners of history? The Incas, while not democratic, had a strong central bureaucracy, a well-run state, a flourishing culture, and wealth fueled by a remarkable degree of trade within its far-flung empire. But the Spanish imposed their bureaucracy and their God for one reason and one reason alone: to extract the New World's riches for the benefit of the motherland. Corruption was institutionalized from the beginning; unlike the British, who paid their tax collectors salaries, Spanish colonial tax collectors actually *paid* the crown for the honor. Implicit in this arrangement was the assumption, of course, that the tax collectors would make up the difference, and then some, by squeezing a little extra out of the populace. Staggering income inequality was also a legacy of the Spanish, who preferred to keep the indigenous majority as poor and uneducated as possible to stave off a rebellion. It was not a coincidence that nearly all of the rich people I knew (and there were few) were relatively light-skinned and nearly all of the poor people I knew were relatively dark-skinned. And the Spanish religion played its role as well, pacifying the poor with the notion that suffering in this world will be rewarded with riches in the next.

But history is not destiny. Egypt's millennia of prosperity did not prevent it from sinking to be the third-rate power it is today. The Japanese, who raped and pillaged their way through Asia in a totalitarian, xenophobic frenzy, have become one of the most pacifist nations on the planet. America's two hundred year history of slavery and long civil rights struggle culminated in the election of an African-American president. And even in Latin America itself there were a few shining examples: I came away very impressed from a visit to Chile, where free trade in tandem with a progressive, uncorrupt government and an excellent universal education system had led to impressive economic growth and the near-eradication of poverty.

In the sweep of human history, cultures wax and wane both in response to external stimuli—wars, economic shocks, natural disasters—and internal stimuli—great leaders and social movements. Ecuador, unfortunately, was not a good candidate for change. The discovery of a moderate amount of oil had not given much of a boost to the economy, and most of its citizens with the greatest potential for leadership had already left the country. Its own people continually bet against it.

The more I thought about Ecuador, the more I thought about my own country as well—where it had been and where it was going. I felt so very grateful for all of the opportunities I had. I was grateful for the police, who took violence against women seriously, and for our health care system which, maligned as it was, would never let a child die in the waiting room while the doctors watched a soccer game. At the same time, I worried about the direction we were headed. Everywhere, from the talking heads on TV to my MBA classmates, there seemed to be irrational enthusiasm for the buzzwords of the much-vaunted new economic order: "deregulation," "market forces," "globalization." There were no people in this new economic order, only forces. I wasn't against marshaling the power of the markets, but what I was against was turning markets into ends in and of themselves. Markets, after all, exist to serve people. That's why we created them.

I wanted to suggest to these people that if they wanted to get a glimpse of their fabled deregulated, pro-business, no-social-services paradise, they should take a trip to Ecuador. They should take a good long look at what it means to surrender completely to the forces of a free market run on cold hard cash, where people are worth their salaries and no more and people die quietly, without protest, when they don't have ten dollars for a bottle of medicine. I wanted to ask them how many of my students it would be "socially efficient" to have die as a result of being run over by unregulated buses or left to die in a waiting room because doctors are not required to attend to dying patients, especially when they know they might not get paid.

I wanted to ask them to calculate the value of Oscar's life and to let me know when they had an answer.

Time truly is a healer. A year after my return, I found that I could no longer muster quite the same anger every time someone mentioned Ecuador. My beliefs had not changed, but my bitterness had faded considerably. I dreamed much less frequently about Ecuador, and when I did, it was not always a nightmare. Other images began creeping into my dreams, of the lovably asymmetrical hearts adorning the patio the night of the Valentine's Day dance, of the marker-sellers on the rusty buses, of the raised hands of my eager *nivelación* boys, of pink eraser shavings coating a scratched-up floor, of squealing girls riding escalators. I would awake from these dreams with the taste of *tomate de árbol* and *chirimoya* juice on my tongue and the words to a *Juanes* song on my lips.

News from Ecuador trickled in now and then. Madre Kathy was attacked and robbed by four young men in the colonial quarter in the middle of the day, but luckily didn't suffer any serious physical injuries. Hot William's mother passed away, and Hot William married a volunteer and moved to Arizona. Susana finally wrangled a visa out of the American Embassy and went to Iowa to finish her religious formation.

President Lucio sacked the members of the Supreme Court, provoking a Constitutional crisis, and brought Bucaram, the ex-president with a Batman complex, back from exile. Massive riots ensued, Lucio declared a state of emergency, and the legislature retaliated by voting 60-2 to remove Lucio from office. Lucio skulked out of the Presidential Palace in the middle of the night, sought asylum at the Brazilian Embassy, and then finally left the country after a standoff at the airport with enraged Ecuadorians blockading the runway.

It was during all of this that Paul decided to come to D.C. for a visit. "Have you seen the pictures of the riots in front of the Palacio del Gobierno?" he asked one day as we sat in a dark, smoky bar.

"Yeah. Scary, huh? To think we walked past that square so many times."

"I think I recognized one of my students in the pictures. A girl throwing rocks at the soldiers. Maybe not, but there was something about that face that was so familiar." He swilled his beer for a moment and then suddenly leaned towards me. "Guess who I saw when I went back to the Center?"

"Jefferson."

He squinted and thought for a moment. "Yeah, I think Jefferson was still around. But I was thinking of someone else."

"Raúl."

"Yeah, he was still around. Maureen, think who you wouldn't expect to be there."

"I don't know."

"Darwin! Can you believe it? I never thought that kid would make it. Never. Not in a million years. I was sure he would have been kicked out by now or drifted off on his own."

I pictured the Atari falling out of his pants with a thud, the various cheeky marriage proposals, his tear-stained Galápagos T-shirt. And then I remembered the day the new and improved Darwin came to class, with his new pencils, his new notebook and his new studious attitude. Maybe, I thought, just maybe, he is the leader Ecuador is waiting for. "Actually," I said, smiling, "I'm not that surprised." And in that instant, Ecuador became not only a place of darkness, but also of possibility.

ABOUT THE AUTHOR

Maureen Klovers has held numerous positions in government, including a stint as a U.S. intelligence officer. She also served as a political commentator on DC 101's talk radio show *Neighborhood Stuff* from 2000 to 2002.

Ms. Klovers has traveled extensively in the United States, Europe, China, India, and Latin America. She's hiked the Inca Trail to Machu Picchu, been escorted through a Bolivian prison by a German narco-trafficker, and fished for piranhas in Venezuela.

She received a Bachelor of Arts in International Relations (with a focus on Latin American politics) from the College of William and Mary in 1999 and a Master's of Public Policy and Master's of Business Administration from Georgetown University in 2006. This is her first book.